Hevva!

Luggers laid at Leland in the 30's

Herb Harris
1965

Hevva!

Cornish fishing in the days of sail

by

Keith Harris

TWELVEHEADS PRESS

TRURO 2010

TWELVEHEADS PRESS

First published 1983. This edition published by Twelveheads Press 2010
ISBN 978 0 906294 71 0
British Library Cataloguing-in-Publication Data.
A catalogue record for this book is available from the British Library.
Printed by R. Booth Ltd, Penryn, Cornwall.

FOREWORD

The enormous advances in technology which have taken place during the past hundred years have changed the Cornish inshore fishing industry almost out of recognition. The picturesque sailing luggers of yesteryear have given place to powered craft equipped with highly sophisticated instruments for detecting fish shoals, with radios and other marvellous aids to efficiency and safety at sea. Indeed, the modern fishing vessel has proved so competent at its task that fish stocks around the coasts have become seriously depleted, a striking instance of man becoming too clever and ingenious for his own good. The danger confronting the industry's future is plain for all to see. The ancient and once great pilchard seine fishery disappeared around sixty to eighty years ago. The herrings have almost gone from our coasts, whilst even mackerel are far less plentiful than they once were. If restraint in fishing and strict conservation measures are not rigorously applied the sea could become a virtual desert and the fisherman as extinct a species as the creatures he once pursued.

With so many changes having taken place in the industry, it is fascinating to take a nostalgic glimpse at those ancient, traditional methods which were still being followed well into the present century. In the following pages, Keith Harris, who has made a detailed study of the subject, takes the reader on a journey into the past: when Cornish harbours such as Newlyn, St Ives, Mevagissey and Looe, were crowded with brown-sailed luggers, and the fishermen who sailed them relied on inherited skills and specialized local knowledge in the pursuit of their often dangerous calling. He has lovingly described their boats; the simple yet beautifully designed gear they used; the long journeys they made under sail to Ireland and the North Sea in the wake of the migrant herring; the shell fisheries; the iniquitous tithe system by which fishermen had to give a tenth of their hard-won catch to the local church or landowners; steam power in fishing boats; rhymes, sayings, superstitions and poems connected with the Cornish fisheries; the Sunday-fishing controversy at St Ives and Newlyn; disasters and loss of life at sea; famous voyages by famous fishing boats; and descriptions of the principal edible types of fish which occur in Cornish waters.

Mr Harris has produced a well-researched and attractively written and illustrated account of Cornish fishing which will form a valuable record of that industry and a fitting memorial to the brave and enterprising men who worked in it.

Cyril Noall

BIBLIOGRAPHY

Carter, C. *Cornish Shipwrecks – North Coast.*

Carter, C. and Larne R. *Cornish Shipwrecks – South Coast.*

Hamilton Jenkins, A. K. *Cornwall and Its People.*

H.M.S.O. *An Account of the Fishing Gear of England and Wales.*

Ivey, W. F. *Wrecks Around Our Coast.*

Lamb, Ted. *The Penguin Book of Fishing.*

March, Edgar I. *Sailing Drifters.*

Morton Nance, R. *A Glossary of Cornish Sea Words.*

Noall, Cyril. *Cornish Seines and Seiners.*

Noall, Cyril. *Harvey's Two Hundred Years of Trading.*

Noall, Cyril. *Tales of Cornish Fishermen.*

Oliver, A. S. *Boats and Boatbuilding in Cornwall.*

Science Museum Publications. *British Fishing Boats and Coastal Craft.*

Wilcocks, J. C. *The Sea Fisherman.*

Newspapers:

The Cornishman;

The Mourne Observer;

The West Briton;

The Western Morning News.

CONTENTS

LIST OF ILLUSTRATIONS
in order of appearance

CHAPTER ONE

INTRODUCTION
AND BACKGROUND

Edible fish can be roughly divided into two main groups: demersal, those fish that live on the sea bed; and pelagic, those that live near the surface. Each type requires an entirely different method of fishing. For the fish on the surface to be caught commercially, they are usually meshed in a curtain of nets which hangs a few fathoms down from the sea's surface. The demersal fish are caught either on hooks, which have been in use since time immemorial, or by the more recent innovation of trawling. Netting and the making of nets is mentioned in both Testaments of the Bible and was a method of fishing certainly known and used by the ancient Egyptians and many earlier civilizations. Discoveries in Roman camps reveal that fishermen of two thousand years ago would learn little from the design of modern hooks.

The adoption of the Christian faith, with its decrees calling for abstinence from eating flesh on certain days, must have been one of the greatest incidental market boosts ever. In the town of St Ives, which caught, cured, exported and survived largely thanks to the humble pilchard, the reliance on the fish was commemorated in the following couplet:

Here's a health to the Pope
And may he repent,
And lengthen six months
The term of his Lent.
It's always declared
Betwixt the two poles
There's nothing like pilchards
For saving of souls.

Many huge shoals of fish were captured off the coast of St Ives using the pilchard seine-net. One such shoal enclosed and landed in 1851 was estimated to have contained 16,500,000 fish, weighing in at 1,100 tons.

The 'Cod War' in Icelandic waters in 1975-6 and the ongoing disputes with our EU neighbours about limits, quotas and sustainable stocks are not new a new development. As long ago as 1415 the King of Denmark, who had Iceland as part of his territorial sovereignty, complained to the English King Henry V about the conduct of fishermen from the British Isles. By 1585 Queen Elizabeth had been forced to issue an Order in Council which empowered officers to take bonds from fishermen engaged in the Icelandic fishery to ensure their peaceable behaviour. It was not only with overseas competitors that strife and conflict arose. In Penzance in 1896 the local men, strict observers of the Sabbath at that time, were faced with East Coast men repeatedly returning from the fishing grounds on Monday mornings, often after fishing with the locally despised trawl net, and flaunting their ill-gotten gains. One Monday morning in the May of 1896 this situation became more than flesh and blood could tolerate and the Newlyn and Penzance men put out to meet the incoming East Coast fleet with every intention of throwing the Sunday-caught fish back where it had come from. The East Coast men got wind of the planned action and sailed, not for Newlyn, but for Penzance. Not to be robbed of this chance of settling what many considered a provocation too long withstood, the Newlyn men returned to port and, after seizing anything that could serve as a weapon, they marched across the promenade to Penzance and a fierce hand-to-hand fight ensued. The fight was only quelled by the timely arrival of a trainload of urgently telegraphed soldiers from Plymouth.

This last ineffectual outburst signalled the decline of the once great Cornish fleets and, although many struggled on, the changing circumstances — notably the development of the first steam drifter, fishing three miles of net to the lugger's one and, later, the internal combustion engine, spelled the end of the traditional Cornish fishing industry.

The First World War really saw the end of the sailing fishing boat, although many are able to recall with great clarity and pleasure the fleets of sailing luggers in Mount's Bay or at anchor in St Ives Bay in the inter-war years. These boats were in all probability Breton crabbers. Engines such as the sixteen horsepower 'hot bulb' Bolinder and Kelvin engines which, after an initial warm-up with a blowlamp, were started on petrol then run on paraffin, signalled the end of sail, and although the mizzen sail was, and still is, maintained on many fishing boats it was kept as a stabilizing vane rather than a propelling sail. PZ 32, *Cely*, was the first Mount's Bay boat to be fitted with an internal combustion engine, a 'hot pot' Alpha, in about 1910.

Many of the traditional luggers, unable to find crews after the decimation of young men in the trenches in the 1914–18 war, never left their winter lay-up berths at Lelant or the old harbour at Newlyn. Many were broken up and burnt in situ, most just quietly and sadly rotted where they were and some, the cream of the fleets, were sold —

not to local buyers but to Irish owners in the ports traditionally visited by the Cornish luggers. Many vessels changed the PZ and SS registration numbers for the N of Newry which covered the ports of Annalong, Kilkeel, New Castle, Dundrum, Killough and Ardglas. The Cornish luggers, of course, were no strangers to Ireland in the second half of the last century. William Paynter, a St Ives boat builder, had established a thriving boat building yard at Kilkeel. His apprentice, John Mackintosh, carried on from him and between them they built many Cornish style luggers for the Irish market. This yard was later run by W 'Bill' Quinn who retired in 1995. One of Paynter's Kilkeel built boats, the *Mary Joseph*, a 51 foot lugger was first registered in Kilkeel with the number N 55 in 1877. She was still in daily use carrying on her old trade, over a hundred years later, although her sails had long since given way to diesel engines. Following Paynter's arrival in 1876 in the lugger *Wanderer*, which he subsequently sold, many St Ives boats made the voyage to new owners, among them *Guiding Star*, built in Penzance in 1878 and weighing 31 tons; *Mermaid*, built in St Ives in 1885 and used in fishing until 1922; *St Mary*, built in St Ives in 1872; and *Snowdrop*, built in St Ives in 1877, a 44 foot lugger weighing 21 tons.

The following ill-fated trio of ex-Cornish luggers were shelled by a German U-boat, *UB64* Capt Otto von Schrader, on 30 May 1918 along with nine other local fishing boats. Capt Schrader ordered the men to leave the boats before he sank them, and even used the submarine to ferry the crews of the vessels with no jolly-boat to the fishing boats *Moss Rose* and *Mary Joseph* which ferried them safely to harbour. The ex-Cornish luggers which were sunk were: *Never Can Tell* built in St Ives in 1881, 50ft overall weighing 31 tons; *Cyprus* built in St Ives, 47ft overall weighing 35 tons; *Lloyd* built in Penzance in 1887 and formerly a very fast lugger.

Another submarine fatality was the St Ives lugger *Mary Anne*. She was sunk after a U-boat skipper apologetically ordered her captain, Matt Stevens, and crew into the jolly-boat. On returning to port, Captain Stevens ordered a new boat which he named *Sheerness* after the steamship that had rescued him and his crew. *Sheerness* remained at St Ives until 1969 when she was sold as a pleasure boat on the East Coast.

In 1915 the Mousehole lugger *Children's Friend* was fired on by a German submarine. She was fishing near the Scillies at the time but, with the aid of a favourable wind and a newly installed engine, she was able, despite further shots, to escape damage and make the St Mary's harbour in safety. A few years later *Children's Friend* was sold to Irish owners and remained fishing until at least 1942. Not that this long working life was unusual. *Peace and Plenty* built in St Ives in 1886 finally retired from her life of toil in 1952. The *Uncle Tom* was built in

St Ives in 1883 and worked as a sailing lugger till 1920. She was still in commission in Irish waters in 1983. So was the *Water Lily* which was built by Henry Trevorrow in 1881, the fastest lugger ever built in Cornwall. She was bought from the Perkins family in St Ives before the First World War for the cost of £150 complete, and is still fishing. The *Amelia Jane* built in St Ives in 1882, the *Arethusa* built in St Ives in 1872 and which survived until at least the 1930s, the *Francis Russell* built in 1883, and boats such as the Porthleven built *Rising Sun* and *Ellen Constance*, already with a motor installed in 1911, also of Porthleven, all made the journey across the Irish Sea to new owners. *Ellen Constance* was once owned by Lord Kilmorey in 1930. Another of Henry Trevorrow's boats which survived, this time in Cornwall, is the St Ives lugger *Barnabas* which, through the Maritime Trust and generosity of Peter Cadbury, has been totally restored and can be seen most of the sailing season in Falmouth.

Barnabas SS634 was built in 1881 for Barnabas Thomas of St Ives. She was given the number 634SS when first registered, the port letters SS for St Ives coming after her number indicating she was a second class pilchard driver. The number 634 was chosen because it was the number of the hymn 'Will your anchor hold' in the Methodist Hymn Book. She was later re-registered as a first class mackerel driver and her port letters moved to prefix her number. *Barnabas* remained in the Thomas family for 73 years and had three generations of Thomas' as her skippers. In 1954 she was sold and converted as a yacht in Falmouth. Fourteen years later she was recognised as a rare surviving example of a Cornish lugger and was purchased by the Maritime Trust. In 1980 she undertook a major refit. The Cornish Maritime Trust, founded in 1989, adopted *Barnabas* as its flagship. The Heritage Lottery Fund provided funding for a major restoration in 2005, undertaken by R. Cann & Sons of Totnes. The restoration took 9 months and involved a major rebuild from and including the keel upwards. On 10 July 2006 *Barnabas* was relaunched and two months later she once again sailed into St Ives harbour.

CHAPTER TWO
DEVELOPMENT OF THE LUGGER

The single square sail set on a midship mounted mast, dates from the dawn of civilization and its operation was as simple as its probable inspiration. The rig consisted of a yard, square to the mast when running before the wind, and braced up when tacking or reaching. It is easy to imagine some skin-clad forefather discovering that standing up in his dug-out and holding his cloak outstretched with the wind behind him was a great deal easier than paddling, and to construct a substitute body and outstretched arms, i.e. a mast and yard with an attached hide, was even better. Thus established, the basic one square sail to each mast, although altered to suit individual preferences, changed hardly at all until the advent of the Dutch herring buss in the fifteenth century. The single square sail and mast, which had survived since the days of the Pharoahs, gave way to the newly introduced fashion of two or three masts each with a square sail and topsail. With so many masts it was often necessary to brace the yards up, and on a tack with the yards peaked up and the tacks sheeted down, the sails resembled lugs.

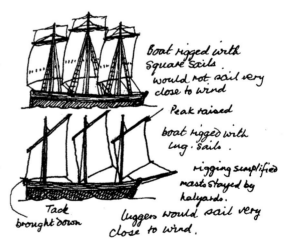

Boat rigged with square sails. would not sail very close to wind

Peak raised boat rigged with lug. sails.

rigging simplified masts stayed by halyards.

luggers would sail very close to wind.

Tack brought down

Further developments did not mean a great deal of alteration. The yards were merely brought inside the rigging and then slung fore and aft, with the point of balance altered to about a third from the fore-end instead of it being literally balanced in the middle. This resulted in a quadrilateral sail with the luff shorter than the leach — the lug sail had come into being.

The French developed the lugger almost to perfection in the form of the Chasse-Maree. This development was not lost on the French Navy and, during the Napoleonic Wars, a large number of Chasse-Marees became privateers. With a crew of up to seventy-five men and armed with up to ten cannons they were a craft to be feared and reckoned with, as many craft plying the Channel found out to their peril.

No doubt contacts made by Cornish fishermen, ever quick to appreciate a fine turn of speed and good handling abilities, and an appreciation of how these qualities could be put to a more profitable use than fishing, led to more Cornishmen adopting the rig.

It soon became apparent that their success as barges for contraband had not escaped the attention of the Preventive men. Because the smugglers' craft had sacrificed all to carrying capacity and speed in her design, new laws governing the ratio of beam to draught and overall

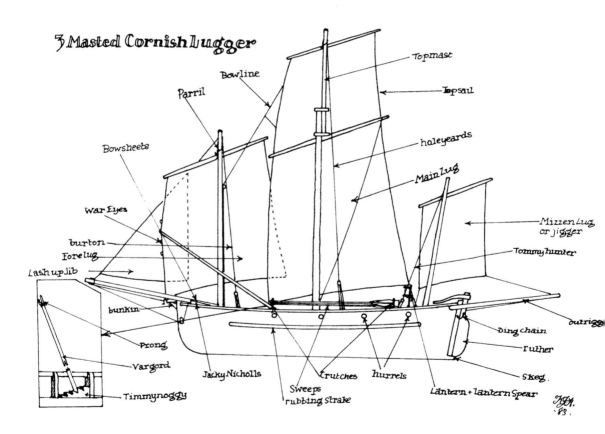

3 Masted Cornish Lugger

length (perhaps the first handicap and rating system) were hastily introduced. Any craft found to be violating such regulations were seized by the Preventive men and, as was the fate of the *Fox* of Cawsand reported in the *West Briton*, 6 November 1840, they were sawn into three parts. No doubt the activities of the smuggler have been romanticized, but as well as the *Fox* of Cawsand, Lieutenant Drew of the *Harpy* managed to apprehend eleven 'fair traders', whilst a further eleven had cause to throw at least part of their cargo overboard in order to effect their escape while he was on station during 1840.

The basic design of the lugger, once established, changed only marginally until its final demise was hastened by the internal combustion engine. The advent of steam power and the development of the railway in the late 1800s did have the effect of increasing the number of markets for fish, but speed was crucial if the day's catch was to catch the train! It was this quest for speed which, more than smuggling or any other consideration, resulted in the abandonment of the rounded hulls, the generous beam and flat floors of the traditional lugger, for the sleek yacht-like hulls. Gone forever was the old 'conger-tailed and cod-headed' appearance of the older boats with their bluff bowed entrance and sharp runs aft. Whilst, aloft, the sailmakers' craft became an art, and the quest to develop a good cut of sails to maximize the fine underwater lines got under way.

To the layman, one lugger was much like another, usually a tarred black hull with her home-port numbers and a couple of strakes picked out in white, topped off with a suit of sails which were any shade of tan through to near black, depending on how long or how often they had been tanned with the cutch used to preserve the nets and ropes. However, a fisherman could tell at a glance where a boat hailed from. Each port, over the years, developed its own characteristics essential to the conditions of their home port. Thus the luggers from Looe, Polperro, Fowey and Mevagissey were built with square transoms, whilst the St Ives, Penzance and Newlyn boats were invariably double-enders, i.e. pointed at both bow and stern. Also the rounded counter of a Porthleven-built boat would be immediately distinguishable from that of a boat from Lowestoft and so on. What a delight they must have been, when compared to today's glass-reinforced plastic and foam sandwich, mass-produced, factory-assembled, little boxes, that are, in the words of the song:

All built out of ticky-tacky,
and all look just the same!

CHAPTER THREE

THE WEST CORNWALL LUGGER

The luggers built on the West Cornwall peninsula were basically pilchard drivers or half-decked boats, and the larger fully-decked mackerel driver capable of staying at sea for days if necessary, and designed to safely work a lifetime in the turbulent waters to the west of Land's End. Owing to the lack of plans or written records, little of any detail is known of the West Cornwall luggers prior to the mid-nineteenth century. Most building done before this period, and indeed much of it done until the early twentieth century, was done by eye and with the use of a half model.

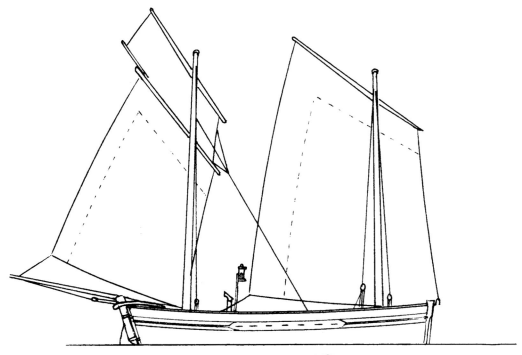

A St. Ives Mackerel Driver Circa 1870

Mackerel Drivers leaving Penzance.

R. Morris

The pilchard driver was built in 1870 for an average cost, ready for sea, of £120. This was for a boat approximately 28 feet long with a 9½ feet beam, a depth of 5 feet 10 inches in the bow and 6 feet 8 inches in the stern. The masts were $6\frac{3}{4}$ inches in diameter foremast and $5\frac{3}{4}$ inches diameter mizzen. Her hull would have been constructed with 2 inch oak for the bilges and the rest in 1 inch Norwegian balk. The hull alone could have been purchased in 1870 for £45.

The mackerel driver was a much bigger boat in every respect usually with an overall length of 45–48 feet probably a 14–15 feet beam and an inside depth of 6 feet 6 inches. The foremast for such a ship would have measured in the region of 40 feet from deck to truck and measured 10 inches in diameter at its step. The outrigger boom for the mizzen sail would have measured 30 feet of which 20 feet would have been outboard. Early mackerel drivers were fitted with a hand capstan but later vessels had a steam-operated windlass. A boat such as this, oak, planked with a yellow pine deck, grown-oak frames on an elm keel, with irons on all her bend planks, would have set a prospective buyer back around £200 complete.

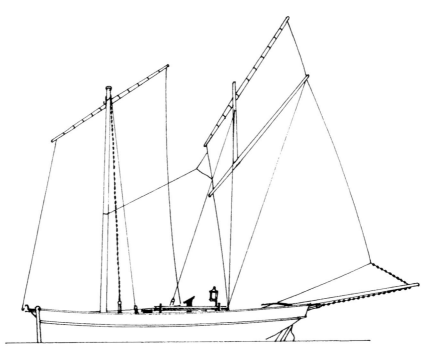

A Counter Sterned Mounts Bay
Mackerel Driver Circa 1890

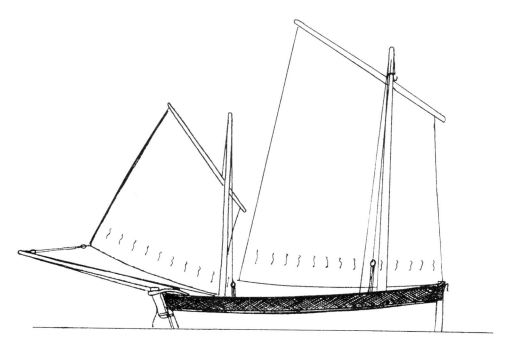

A St. Ives Pilchard Driver Circa 1900

The main difference between boats built by such men as William Paynter of St Ives and James R. Wills of Penzance was the fact that the luggers of St Ives were much heavier and rounder size for size than the Mount's Bay boats. Also the St Ives boats were ballasted so they had all their weight amidships and drew more water aft, whereas the Newlyn boats tended to be deeper forward and lighter aft. The rounded bilges enabled the St Ives boats to sit upright on the dried-out harbour bottom. Legs such as those used to support the finer Mount's Bay hulls would have been useless in the ebbing, surging tide at St Ives and broken legs would have probably been the lightest damage done under such exposed conditions.

The St Ives boats could also be recognized by the cut of their sails. They stepped the mast closer to the bow and the sails were cut much narrower and taller. The St Ives men also preferred a longer outrigger and did not use the jenny boom on the foot of the big mizzen. Nor did the St Ives men take up the Mount's Bay practice of setting a triangular 'watch' mizzen. The Mount's Bay boats used raft irons whereas the St Ives men never did.

In building the boat, as previously mentioned, the builder would work to rough instructions as to length, overall depth and beam.

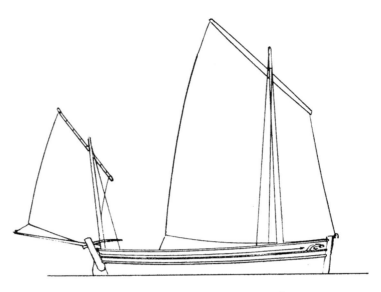

Mounts Bay Pilchard Driver
Circa 1900

Plans, if used, were seldom referred to, as a good builder would have all the boat's lines in his head. Once stem and stern posts had been erected on the American-elm keel, and a couple of ribands of light timber had been tacked around a few moulding frames, work would commence. The frames of oak were set up vertically, so upon completion the launched boat's frames would all take on a rake aft. The forward frames, tapered to wedge points, and were bolted to the deadwoods; the after frames butted onto the deadwood and were then bolted to chocks aft of the foot of each respective frame. Midship frames were made up in sections, the lower floor section moulded to the shape of the bilge. On top of these were bolted the 'foot icks' which extended around the turn of the bilge and up the top sides. On top of these, making in all five pieces per frame, came the timber heads. The spacing altered from builder to builder, but as a rule of thumb on a 42 foot boat there would usually be 33 timbers.

The timber used included American-elm for keels and all bendable work. Beams, stem and sternpost, along with knees, would have been in oak; hull planking, depending on the finances, could be white, yellow or pitch pine or oak; yellow planking was chosen as decking because of its straight grain, lack of knots and impermeability and also good wearing properties. Presumably this is why masons' wooden trowels for plastering are made from the same wood. Spars would have been made from spruce, fir or yellow pine. The older boats had washstrakes but later vessels were built with bulwarks 20 inches high, just enough when hauling nets aboard to brace one's knees against!

The hatches were built to the owner's specifications. They were often not put in a central position but, for ease of working, were placed slightly off-centre nearer the starboard side. Hatch coamings were built approximately 6 inches high. Fixed ballast was in the form of concrete laid between the floors mainly under the fish and net rooms, whilst moveable ballast in the form of either iron pigs or granite boulders, or a mixture of both, was stored in the wings. This ballast was enough to bring the lugger to her waterline marks when at a mooring, but could be shifted to the windward side when the vessel was sailing. To minimize the cost of a new boat many skippers would enlist the services of the crew in helping with the more menial tasks involved in her construction.

It was common practice for a skipper requiring a new boat, or an owner wishing to start or add to his fleet, to purchase what timber he required for a hull inclusive of spruce or pine for masts and spars. Having got the timber at a cost of approximately £140, he would then negotiate with local boat builders to have this timber built into his boat at a further cost of £40 or so, working at a usual rate of £1 charged for each foot length of the hull. At Newlyn, as in St Ives and Porthleven, Portreath, Hayle and most other villages, everything was at hand locally. Each village had its own saw-pit for cutting the large timbers down. The saw-pit at Newlyn was on the site of the present Fisherman's Mission. A capstan could be ordered from Newlyn Foundry in Foundry Lane, or from Harvey and Co. at Hayle, and would have cost £10. Any ironwork required could be undertaken by local smiths and was included in the cost of the boat.

Other costs were:

> Navigation lights – iron/zinc plated £1, Copper £1.10s each
> Anchor £1.10s
> Rigging £2
> Fore halyard blocks £3
> Masthead and lower light £1.10s each
> Compass and binnacle £4–£5
> Net roller 10s
> Paint costing 5d–6d per lb – 20lb being required
> Anti-fouling patent paint for the bottom 10s
> Sails: 140yd Foresail £6
>   90yd Mizzen £4.10s
>   35yd Mizzen topsail £2.5s
>   30yd Jib foresail £1.12s. 6d

Richard Trewavas, an eighteenth century poet and fisherman, wrote about the building and launching of his first boat *Minerva*. He described her as 'of carvel build oak planked and finished off with a covering of tar'. *Minerva* was built at St Michael's Mount in 1785 and Trewavas relates that at her launch the assembled company drank to her success and the builder dashed as much as he thought fit of a glassful of drink over her bows before *Minerva* was eased into the water. The advent of Methodism brought with it sobriety and the 'pledge' and this restraint extended even to the launch of a new lugger when the traditional bottle of wine or spirits was commonly replaced with a bottle of spring or Madron Well water. Prior to the arrival of the teetotal crusade led by James Teare from the Isle of Man, a Mousehole launch included tea and launching cake for the crew and builders and a jar or two of beer for those who drank.

The ceremony of a launch usually involved the owner's daughter waiting for the boat to move off the chocks on the slip, then smashing wine or brandy (in the case of the unconverted), or spring or well water (in the case of the abstainers), over the bow iron. The name, usually kept secret until the launch, was bestowed upon the new vessel and a speech to 'success and good luck to the *Mary Jane*', or whatever the name was, followed. It was all over with little or no fuss.

Luggers were paid-up or painted up once a year, usually before going to the North Sea Fishery. The usual form of paying-up on the traditional tar and pitched boats was to take the boat up on the hard and brim her. This took the form of one man going over the hull with a fork, attached to which was a bundle of blazing tar-impregnated rags or nets. He held this against the hull and melted any existing tar and pitch to boiling point. Another man, armed with a three-headed tar brush, came behind him and swept hot tar on to the hot hull, effectively filling all the seams, killing off any marine growth and barnacles attached to the hull, and giving the boat a sealing coat of new pitchy tar. Cornish boats were always very sombre and conservative in colour. Tar was the usual 'paint'. Occasionally the bulwark rail would be painted white, while some boats used a mixture of white and black lead which gave a grey colour. The inner surface of the bulwarks were often painted white with the stanchions picked out in blue. It was sometimes observed that on the companion hatch a blue diamond shape would be painted on a white background. If the colours were reversed this signified the death of the owner and the colours would remain reversed for one year. The masts and spars were either varnished or dressed with pilchard oil.

The West Cornish Luggers were built to last and built to work. The mackerel season began in January and lasted until June. The early season began with boats leaving port and sailing sometimes a hundred

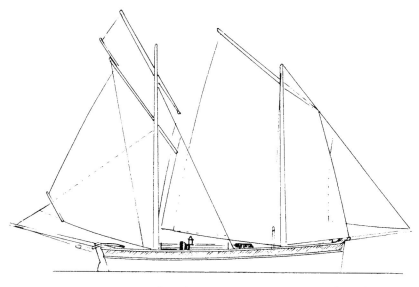

A Mounts Bay Lugger Showing Full Sail Plan

miles west of the Wolf Rock to meet the migrating shoals. These grounds lay in very busy steamer routes and in poor visibility, many a boat and crew was run down by some anonymous steamer driving hell-bent regardless of conditions. From June until August the luggers took on their herring-nets and sailed for the Irish Sea, fishing from southern Irish ports or from the Isle of Man. Many luggers fished the waters as far away as Shetland before making Whitby or Scarborough their base for the North Sea summer fishing. The North Sea fishery lasted from July/August until early October when the fleet would return home to Cornwall. Fast passages were made by many luggers, the 'race' home often taking on the atmosphere of a regatta with much personal pride involved. No sacrifice was too great to achieve another half a knot, even to the point of hauling and lashing the punt on the windward side and having it filled with water so the large driving lugs could be held rather than shortening sail. In 1902 the lugger *Lloyd* covered the six hundred or so miles from Scarborough to St Ives in fifty hours. Her skipper, it is recorded, was a hard man, who would keep his biggest sails up in strong winds, pitch dark night, or foggy weather when more careful men would shorten down. Recorded times of a hundred hours by *British Workman* SS 494 and *T.R.C.* SS 539 for the 850-mile voyage from Peterhead would take some beating by today's racing yachtsmen. Lugger skippers often capitalized on an empty hold by bringing home a cargo of coal or potatoes.

For speed and seaworthiness the luggers of West Cornwall were without peer and the quality of work in their construction is illustrated by their longevity. *Freeman* built in St Ives in 1861 was still at work in County Down, Eire in the 1930s and many of the Porthleven boats built in the 1890s were still working prior to the outbreak of the Second World War. Boats lasting forty or fifty years were not at all uncommon and many survived to become septuagenarians and older.

On reaching their home ports in Cornwall the luggers would then get kitted up for the pilchard fishery. Apart from fishing for pilchards, each man aboard would be equipped with a 50–60 fathom handline with which he would fish for hake. Hake were a great predator on the pilchard shoals and as many as 40,000 fish, sold at a rate of 12s–13s for a 'burn' of 21 fish, were landed at Newlyn after a single night's fishing. After the pilchard season the drivers again changed their nets for mackerel nets and fished either the waters off the Isles of Scilly or went to the east to work the waters near Plymouth and the Eddystone. This period lasted until January when the main season west of the Wolf began in earnest. Just what the fishing industry meant to Cornwall is illustrated by the following figures drawn up in 1827:

Number of seine-nets employed in Cornwall	186
Number of seine-nets not in employment	130
Total	316
Number of drift boats in Cornwall	368
Number of men employed by drift boats	1,600
Number of men employed by seines at sea	2,672
Number of persons employed on shore but directly with the fishery	6,350
Total number of persons employed	10,622

By the year 1849 Penzance alone had registered 300 boats employing 2,000 hands. In 1859, excluding the 320 boats St Ives fishermen had registered for operating the seine fishery, she had 110 vessels employing 600 crewmen and boys engaged in drift fishing. Sadly within seventy years the number of boats, according to Olsens 1930 edition, fell to a mere 59 boats from both ports, with no luggers or sailing vessels at all.

Chapter Four

Luggers of east Cornwall

The East Cornish fishing fleet hailing from the ports of Mevagissey, Fowey, Polperro and Looe were easily distinguishable from the West Cornwall fleet because of their transom sterns. Their differences could be closer defined by the fact that those boats from Mevagissey favoured a backward-raking sternpost, whilst vessels from Looe and Fowey were more upright. Smaller boats known locally as 'gaffers' came mostly from Polperro and closely resembled the Truro river oyster boats, with the difference that the mainsail on the Polperro craft carried no boom. At Mevagissey they were called 'toshers' and an increase in harbour fees for boats over the length of 20 feet resulted in the canny local fishermen ordering boats measuring 19 feet 11 inches.

These vessels were in the main rigged with only one mast and single lug sail. The larger driving boats measuring 30–40 feet, apart from sternposts, were practically identical regardless of home port. Some owners went in for luggers built with counter-sterns but none remained permanently in the area. Various experiments with the rig were made and rejected, the mizzen topsail being one. Most owners and skippers rigged the boats with only a main and mizzen sail, a dipping lug on the foremast and a standing lug on the mizzen. Some boats carried jib sails carried on a short bowsprit or 'bospard', these were of three diminishing sizes known as the balloon jib of forty square yards, a working jib of twenty square yards and a storm job or 'smiter' of seventeen square yards.

The East Cornish boats too went to the North Sea for the summer herring fishery. This traditional migration was started in 1863 by the 32 foot Mevagissey lugger *Band of Hope*. In contrast to the vessels of today with their luxurious appointments, the *Band of Hope* and her sister ships were completely open except for a cuddy under the foredeck. This shelter, nine feet from the bow and tapering to the bow, was only 3 feet 6 inches high. This was the only shelter and living accommodation aboard for the four man crew. Hard conditions bred hard men. How else would they have survived?

The fishing for the East Cornish fleet came in four seasons: First the crabbing season with the men going crabbing in the mornings, lifting

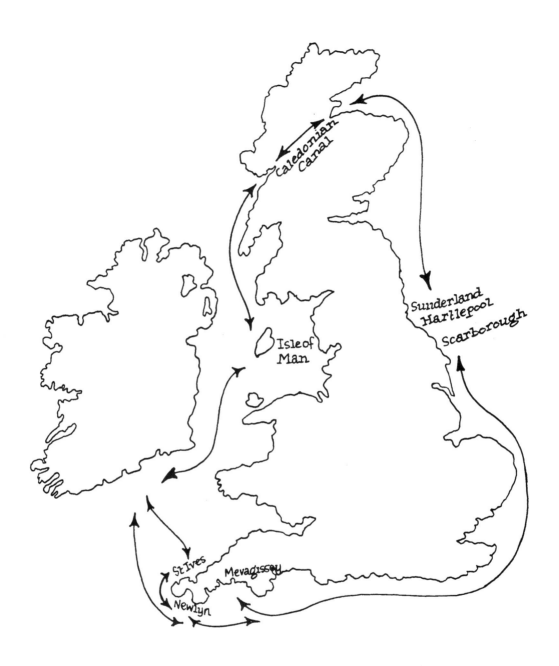

Caledonian Canal

Sunderland
Hartlepool
Scarborough

Isle of Man

St Ives

Mevagissey

Newlyn

Map showing Extent of Usual Range Of
Cornish Mackerel Drivers.

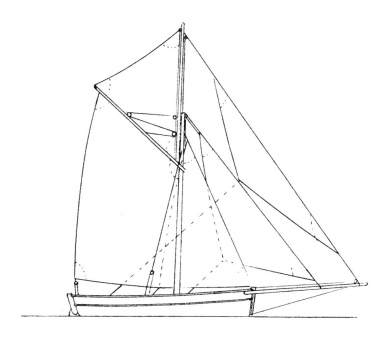

A Polperro Gaffer Circa 1900

and rebaiting pots. They landed and stored their catch till numbers or price was at a peak, spending the afternoons catching up with maintenance and cleaning jobs about the boat and her gear. Some owners used their boats to collect seaweed which was sold to farmers as manure, while other skippers took on board long-lines containing six or seven hundred hooks. As the season developed, the mackerel nets were placed on board and the boats worked the waters off the Eddystone. Fishing and landing on the same day meant that mackerel could reliably be bought and sold in a fresh state locally. Crew men as well as customers had to pay for any fish taken home. The mackerel season continued until June when the boats were paid up and got ready for the pilchard season. This could be a very profitable time if conditions were right. It is recorded that one East Looe fisherman in 1812 received £400 for fresh fish caught in one week, a tremendous amount of money when one could buy a new boat ready for sea with all gear aboard for about £100 at this time. As the season wore on the pilchards would come nearer and nearer to land and by harvest time would reinforce the saying: 'When the corn is in the shock, then the fish are on the rock'. It was during this time that the large company-owned seines were worked. The seine-net fishery represented a great capital outlay. In 1827 it was estimated that the cost of fitting out a seine was about £800, whereas the fitting out of a drift fishing lugger was about £6 for a fleet of nets and £100–£140 for the boat. Every part of Cornwall depended on a successful seine season. Most families would salt down from 1,500 to 2,000 fish to last the winter. Captains of local coastal traders took on enough salted pilchard to feed their crews for the winter. The pilchards were purchased at a rate of about six or seven new pence per hundred fish.

By October the weather would start to deteriorate and some of the pilchard drivers would reduce the number of nets carried and, like their brethren on the West Cornwall boats, the East Cornish fishermen would arm themselves with handlines and fish for hake. A good night's fishing might realize 120–360 fish which then sold at 6d to 7d each. Some boats fished for pilchard and hake all winter whilst others rigged up for the herring fishery, first from Torquay and Brixham, and then from Plymouth and the grounds off Bigbury Bay.

The sailing fleet of East Cornwall declined even more quickly than the fleets of West Cornwall. The County Returns of 1889 show that the registered East Cornish Fleet was 218 boats in number and employed 765 men and 58 boys. Within fifty years, the Olsen's Register of 1936 shows, the number of boats bearing the FY registration of Fowey had fallen to 36, not one of them a sailing lugger!

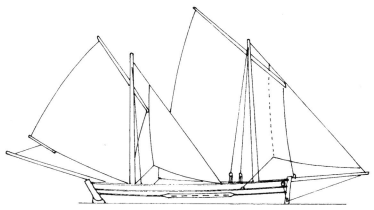

Mevagissey Lugger Circa 1900

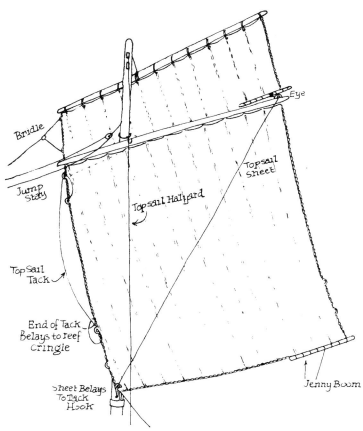

Bridle

Eye

Jump Stay

Topsail Sheet

Topsail Halyard

Top Sail Tack

End of Tack
Belays to reef
Cringle

Sheet Belays
To Tack
Hook

Jenny Boom

Mizzen Mast Details

Rigging Details

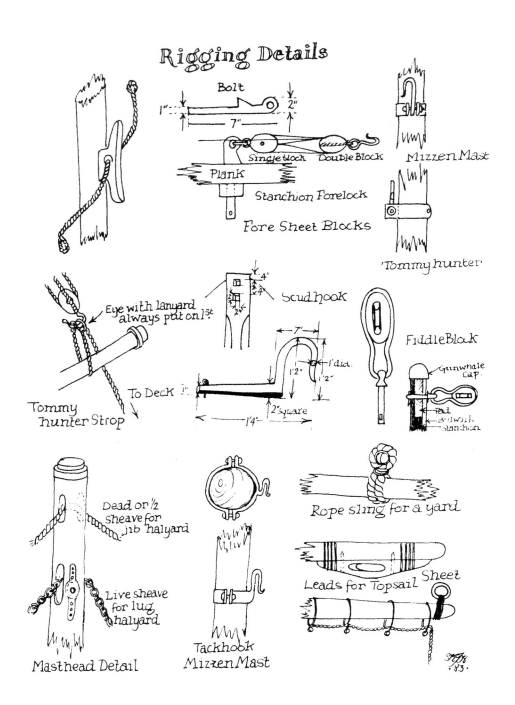

Bolt

1" 7" 2"

Single block   Double Block

Plank

Stanchion Forelock

Fore Sheet Blocks

Mizzen Mast

'Tommy hunter'

Eye with lanyard always put on 1st

Scud hook

Tommy hunter Strop

To Deck 1"

4"
4"
2"

7"
1' dia.
1' 2"   1' 2"
2" square
1' 4"

Fiddle Block

Gunwhale cap.

Pad or washer stanchion

Dead or ½ Sheave for jib halyard

Live sheave for lug halyard

Masthead Detail

Tackhook Mizzen Mast

Rope sling for a yard

Leads for Topsail   Sheet

Fishers in Mevagissey Harbour.

Keith Harris 87

MAUN OR BASKET CONTAINING LONG LINE, TROT, BULTER OR SPILLER

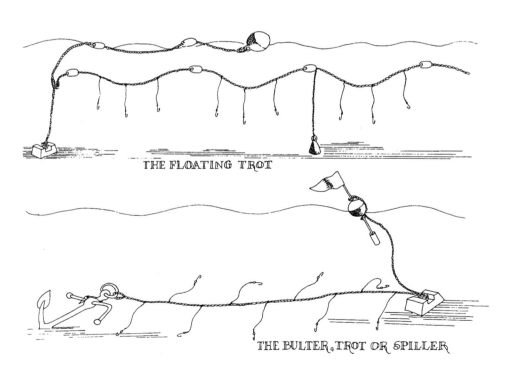

THE FLOATING TROT

THE BULTER, TROT OR SPILLER

CHAPTER FIVE

HANDLINE FISHING

Handline fishing, or whiffing as it is called when talking of the mackerel fishery, was a method used by all classes of fishing vessels from the gigs to the largest mackerel drivers. Its principal virtue is that it was simply the cheapest gear available. In its most basic form it consists of a cater or frame on which the line is wound. The line itself is usually no more than 40 fathoms long with a number of hooks and swivels and a heavy lead sinker. Before the invention of nylon and other synthetics, gut was used to make traces, but before that and from time immemorial the snoods of the fisherman's line would have to be spun or twisted to give them greater strength and durability. Various materials were used, depending on what fish the line was designed to catch. Cobbler's shoe thread was used for whiting lines, whereas some favoured silk for mackerel snoods – even horsehair was used for some lines. A simple machine, known as a Nossil Cock was often employed to twist the chosen fibres into a serviceable snood. Two people were required to operate a nossil cock; one to pull the endless cord, whilst the other, either with a stick or with his fingers, prevented the strands from twisting too rapidly. The man with the cord would stop as soon as the strands had twisted as far as the spread of the hooks would allow. The lead weights attached to the bottom of the nossils would be allowed to spin on until their momentum was spent, then the lay of the nossil was equalized and consolidated by pulling a piece of soft leather gripped tightly around the nossil, along its length. Only when a piece of line had a hook attached to it would it be called a snood. Prior to that it was known as a nossil.

The main fish sought by the handliners was and is the mackerel, although in the last decade technology has changed this basic method out of all recognition from the former simple cater and feathers technique. The gurdy or handlining reel was the first innovation; the gurdy is in effect a large fishing reel, often made locally and employing either specially made reels or adapted car wheels. The reel is secured to the rail of the rail of the boat and cranked much in the same way as the hurdy-gurdy, after which, presumably it is named. Next came the use of strippers which were a system of rollers, first large, widely-spaced

The Nossil Cock or Fishermans spinner

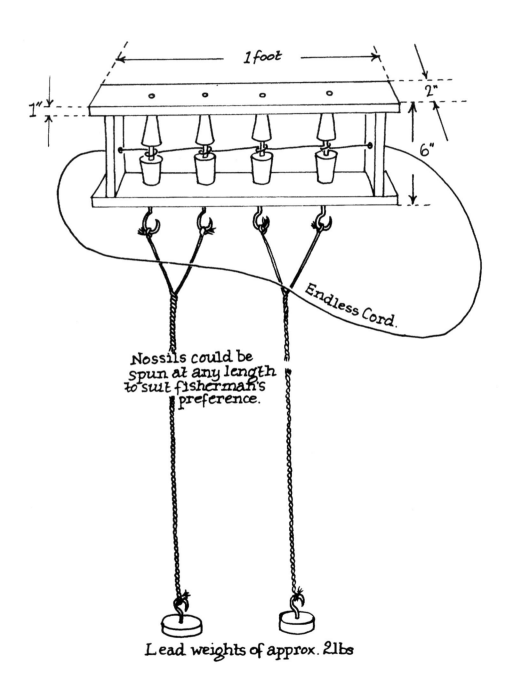

1 foot

2"

1"

6"

Endless Cord.

Nossils could be spun at any length to suit fisherman's preference.

Lead weights of approx. 2lbs

Details of Gurdy and Fish Stripper Used In Hand Line Mackerel Industry

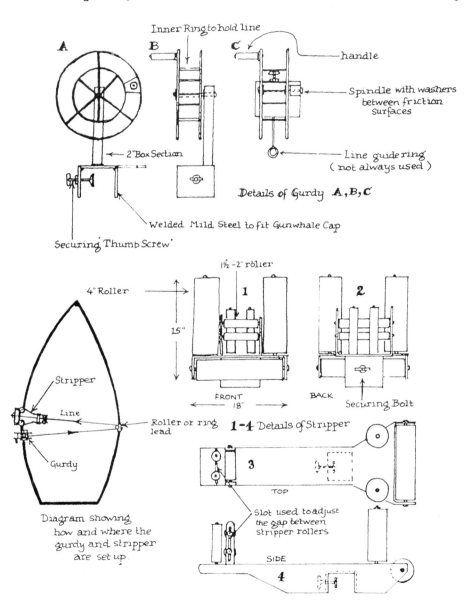

Inner Ring to hold line

A

B

C

handle

Spindle with washers between friction surfaces

Line guide ring (not always used)

2" Box Section

Details of Gurdy A, B, C

Welded Mild Steel to fit Gunwhale Cap

Securing Thumb Screw

4" Roller

1½ - 2" roller

1

2

15"

FRONT
18"

BACK

Securing Bolt

Stripper

Line

Roller or ring lead

Gurdy

1-4 Details of Stripper

3

TOP

Slot used to adjust the gap between stripper rollers

SIDE

4

Diagram showing how and where the gurdy and stripper are set up.

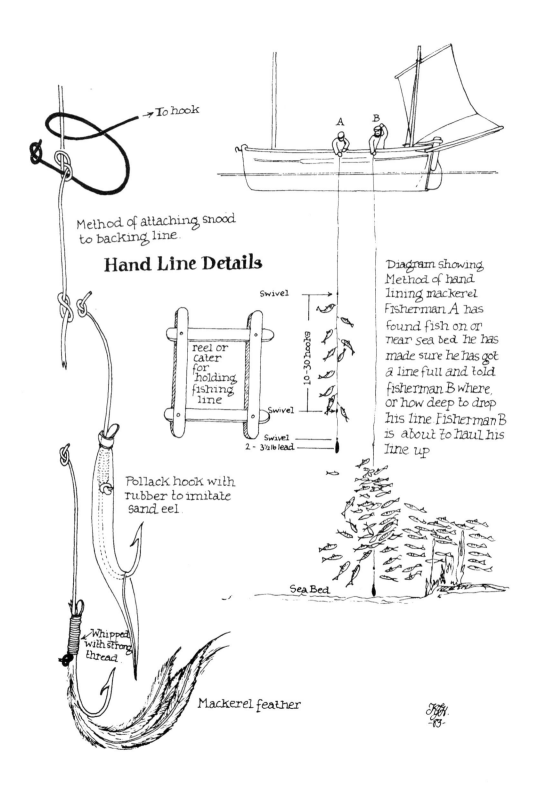

To hook

Method of attaching snood to backing line.

Hand Line Details

reel or cater for holding fishing line

Swivel

10-30 hooks

Swivel

Swivel
2 - 3½lb lead

Pollack hook with rubber to imitate sand eel.

Whipped with strong thread

Mackerel feather

Diagram showing Method of hand lining mackerel. Fisherman A has found fish on or near sea bed. he has made sure he has got a line full and told fisherman B where, or how deep to drop his line. Fisherman B is about to haul his line up

Sea Bed

ones which directed and eased fish aboard, then smaller, narrowly spaced rollers which allowed only the hooks through and effectively tore the hooks from the fishes mouths – messy, cruel, but devastatingly effective. The last change was to power the gurdy with an hydraulic motor thus converting the gurdy into a mini power-winch.

When the pilchard shoals came around the Cornish coasts in great numbers they were always preyed upon by large shoals of hake. The hake in turn were fished for by handliners using an especially large hook, the shank of which was usually 8 inches long. This ensured that the voracious hakes' needle-sharp teeth were kept well away from the snoods. Haking was always carried out at night and it is recorded that as many as 50 dozen hake and 5000 pilchards were taken in one night's fishing by a crew consisting of four men and a boy. This fishery along with the pilchard has, sadly, disappeared.

Ling and Spur-dogs are still fished for with handlines, as are pollack. The development of marine electronics such as the depth-sounder and recorder have made handlining a commercially viable method of fishing, and good catches of these fish are frequently taken from wrecks and reefs located by such equipment.

CHAPTER SIX

CORNISH GIGS

Luggers were not the only vessels employed in the Cornish fisheries. Inshore, almost every port and cove had a fleet of gigs. The original Cornish Gig was a clinker-built boat of about 25 feet overall and built long and low with a very racey appearance. Indeed, racing for pilotage work was one of the original uses of this boat and it was not an uncommon event for two or more gigs to race many miles with only one crew likely to be the winner – there were, after all, no prizes for second and third place!

The gigs carried a crew of four, three oarsmen and a cox. The oars provided the main form of propulsion with a boat of such low freeboard. Sailing in anything but a light breeze must have been a very tricky operation. Gigs were used as a fast, easily-launched beach boat, and handlining for mackerel and hake was their principal occupation in the fishing industry – although later they were used as mullet seine boats. However, this did not come about until the advent of the internal combustion engine and the change in build and design from clinker to carvel-build and from the narrow to wider transom.

Many West Cornwall ports had a fleet of gigs and a 'pulling' race between rival crews was always a feature of any regatta.

Gigs, although no longer used as pilot boats or fishing vessels, have been preserved, both on mainland Cornwall and in the Scillies, as racing craft. Newquay Rowing Club have six boats. The oldest, aptly named *Newquay*, was built in 1812 and is still going strong. *Newquay*, *Treffry* and *Dove* have recently benefitted from the Heritage Lottery Fund for a programme of restoration work. One of the early gigs, in fact the first six-oared gig, was used as a lifeboat on the North Cornish Coast. Newquay Rowing Club have claims that one such gig is on record as having been rowed almost to Lundy Island in order to secure the pilotage of a schooner bound for Newquay. The Newquay gigs can be seen in action most Thursdays and Sunday evenings throughout the summer.

Rival gig crews from Mousehole would often row across the wide expanse of Mount's Bay and around the Lizard in the hope of intercepting a London steamer calling in at Penzance for barrelled pilchards, the losing crew having no option but to turn around and pull back across the bay for home. Apart from a turn at baling or steering, they would hardly let go of their oars for the whole trip and whether it was rain or shine, fair weather or foul, each had no option other than to grin and bear it and take it as part of the day's work.

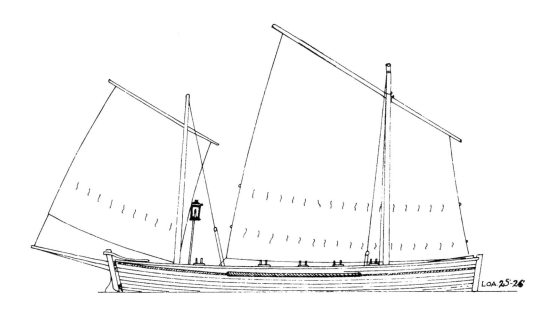

Cornish Gig Showing Sail Plan

CHAPTER SEVEN

SUPPORT INDUSTRIES AND LIVING CONDITIONS

Every cove, port and estuary along the Cornish coast once carried out some kind of fishery. This was born of necessity rather than any other consideration. Villages such as Cadgwith, Portwrinkle, Porthpean, Boscastle, all had active fishing industries and many villages described fishing as their chief industry. Apart from one first-class boat and thirty-five unregistered boats employing fifty-four men and two boys, the port of Gorran also engaged in crabpot-making and boat building; sail-making was the speciality of Par; cask-making was undertaken at St Ives and, if you required ropes and blocks, Fowey was the place. Porthleven, St Mawes, St Ives, Portscatho, Portloe, Polkerris, Polperro, Newlyn, Mousehole, Mevagissey and Looe all supported thriving curing houses; and although Polruan did not build boats, it did repair them. Eels were speared in the Wadebridge area and gives the unquestionable impression that whatever one wanted, if it was in any way connected with the fishing industry, it was to be had here – not in Bristol, Birmingham, or London, but right here on our own doorstep.

When one considers a village such as Porthleven, which in 1889 was described as having a population of 2,300 and out of that total population 373 men and boys were engaged at sea, working on the twelve, first-class boats, 118 second-class boats and twenty-three unregistered boats belonging to the port, whilst ashore the following industries were pursued: ship and boat building, basket-making, box-making, barrel-making, net-making, sail-making and fish-curing, there surely cannot have been an unemployment problem in 1889!

At St Ives in the same year, out of a population of 6,445, no less than 1,060 men and boys, or approximately one-sixth of the total population, were engaged in crewing the town's fishing fleet; whilst ashore the pilchard curing houses, or palaces, as they were locally known, were the chief employer of the town's womenfolk. Yet for all the obvious advantages of a society almost totally self-sufficient, life was not all 'cakes and ale'. Life at sea was unimaginably hard, toilet facilities were non-existent and cooking facilities were crude in any and every sense, often amounting to no more than a hearth hollowed out of a granite block or a box of clay and small pebbles. These old-time fishermen must have been as hard as their native granite. The luxury of a fire was almost unknown, for many skippers feared the constant danger of a fire on board. And if the men were tough, then so were the women. A jouster (a hawker of fish) would cover up to nine parishes which would take the whole day to complete on foot, carrying a burden of close on a hundredweight; comprising about 40lbs of salt in large pockets around her waist and the rest in a cowal or basket on her back.

In the early decades of the nineteenth century living conditions were very poor. A skilled farm labourer earned about 9s per week if he took a tied cottage and about 12s if he had his own accommodation. The standard wage for a surface worker in the mines was never much more than 10s per week, whilst the rent for a cottage with a garden could range, depending on size, from £2.10s to £5 per year.

With fish established as a staple article of diet, it is easy to understand just how much depended on a successful fishery. Every family laid in store 1,000 to 2,000 pilchards, depending on the number of mouths to feed and these were purchased at a rate of six or seven pence for a hundred fish. The fish were then thoroughly washed and cleaned and stacked in rows alternating with a layer of salt in large earthenware pots known as bussas.

Salt, the curing agent in the preservation of pilchards, often proved to be a problem, particularly in the Napoleonic era when the best salt for preserving happened to originate in the Mediterranean countries. This carried an imposed tax of £35 per ton. Before the war the amount needed to salt the winter's supply down equalled 8s–9s or a man's wages for a week. The increase to £1.3s – £1.4s created by the tax often meant going short. Of course, there were always those who found a means of getting around the problem. Salt used in the balking of pilchards in the cellars was tax-exempt and, apart from this source, much salt was smuggled. However, the tax existed officially until hostilities ceased in 1815.

Many families supplemented their meagre wages by extracting fish oil. Train oil from the pressing of pilchards was the most commonly used oil and could be extracted from prime condition fish at a rate of two gallons per hogshead. The best fish for pressing were those caught early in the season by the drift fishermen. Hake livers were also used to render hake oil and this was sold off to shipwrights and blacksmiths at a rate of 3s 7d per gallon. Until the advent of paraffin as a source of lighting, pilchard oil was often used as a cheap but, if one can imagine the smell of hot fish oil, a somewhat aromatic alternative to tallow dips or animal fats. Pilchard oil was burnt for lighting in a lamp known as a chill. In early times a 'stonen chil', or earthenware lamp – a well with one or more lips punch-moulded in the rim and holding half to one pint of oil – was used with wicks or 'purvans' made from the pithy core of a rush. Latterly, chills were made in the local foundries from cast-iron and could be either stood on the table or hung from a nail. Until the last century 'train' or pilchard oil could be purchased in every town, much as paraffin can be bought today. Fishwives would bring in large jars of train oil in exchange for cash or goods and it could be purchased by country folk along with their regular provisions. Thus the humble pilchard lived up to its colourful epithet:

Meat, money and light – all in one night.

The diet of the working man in Cornwall seems to have come in for a good deal of ribald comment. However, according to tradition the Devil never crossed the Tamar into Cornwall for fear of being put into a pasty. The fare on the average Cornishman's table was invariably much more basic than is romantically imagined. One contemporary verse of doggerel describes the Cornish menu and lifestyle thus:

Gurty milk and bearly bread no lack,
Pudden skins and good shaip's chack
A bussa o' salt pelchers, nother o' pork
A good strong stommick, an plenty o' work.

'Gurty milk' was probably a gruel or porridge made of small millet like seeds; 'bearly bread' was bread made from barley flour; 'pudden skins and sheep's chack' probably refer to hogs pudding and brawn made from a sheep's cheek; salt pelchers are obviously pilchards, and the bussa is the jar to preserve them in.

Another rhyme, from the Scillies, illustrates a cheerful outlook on what appears to be less than appetising fare:

Scads an' tates, scads an' tates,
Scads an' tates and conger,
An' they who can''t eat scads and tates
O' they must die of hunger!

Apart from the 'scad' or shad mackerel mentioned in this rhyme, and the conger and pilchards which have also been mentioned, Cornwall seems to have been a great county for preserving practically all kinds of fish.

Listed below are those methods used in the preservation:

Pilchard	Salted, smoked and sold as 'Fairmaids' or 'Fumados' baked with spice and vinegar, canned

Mackerel	Salted, marinated, smoked
Ling	Salted and dried mainly in Scillies
Hake	Salted and dried, exported to Wales and Spain
Whiting	Salted and dried, sold as 'Buckhorn'
Coalfish or Rauning Pollack	Salted
Haddock	Salted or smoked
Cod	Salted or dried, known as 'Tow rag'
Pollack	Salted or dried
Conger	Dried, salted or marinated in vinegar
Skate	Salted and dried, also known as 'Tow rag'
Dog Fish	Salted and used in West Cornwall in 'Morgy pie' and 'Morgy broth'
Dabs and flounders	Salted and dried
Cockles, Mussells, and Oysters	Pickled
Cod and Hake sounds (air bladders) and tongues	These were salted and considered by some to be a delicacy.

The ubiquitous pilchard oil, apart from its use as lamp oil, was also used in leather tanning and as a lubricant for the painting of ships spars. It also found its way into a cheap, coarse paint which was often used to weatherproof the clapboard covering found on many poor Cornish cottages.

In view of the less than epicurian standard of daily fare it is hardly surprising that this couplet was allegedly said as grace before and after meals:

Before the meal: *Lord make us able*
                     to ait what's on the table.
and after the meal: *The Lord be praised*
                     and our stomachs be aised.

CHAPTER EIGHT

PILCHARD FISHING
WITH THE SEINE-NET

The month of July usually heralded the start of the pilchard season, and by the end of the month the majority of seining companies would have their nets and boats ready for sea. The few pilchards, caught to the west of Land's End by drivers fishing for mackerel during the months of May and June, would have been regarded as insignificant in number and therefore disregarded. The main shoals began to appear about the month of July and their arrival was always a matter for conjecture and excitement. The pilchard shoals attracted a great number of larger predatory fish such as the hake which, in turn, were sought after by the long-liners.

The great shoal of pilchards would appear as a stain of red, purple and silver in the water, while overhead flocks of screaming gulls and plummet ing gannets marked their position from the air. On they came, past the Wolf Rock, on until the granite buttresses of Land's End split the shoals, dividing them into two separate bodies. The northern shoal carried on past Sennen, past St Ives, and right up the North Cornish coast. The southern shoal swept into Mount's Bay then round the Lizard and on up channel to Falmouth, Mevagissey and Fowey. The pilchard fishery, thus started, usually lasted four months but occasionally went on into the New Year. Pilchards and harvest-time usually occurred at the same time hence the saying:

Corn up in shock
Fish into rock.

The seine, or sean as some contemporaries spelled it, was considered to be *the* way to catch the pilchard. Laws were passed to ensure that drivers of mackerel and pilchards should not break up the huge mass of fish before they reached the shore. Driving boats were forced to obey fishing law which required them to be at least three miles offshore before they shot any nets. The seiners were usually a company of men who collectively owned what is comprehensively called a seine, amounting to three boats and two nets and pilchard cellars ashore. The gross cost for such an enterprise was approximately £800, a fearsome amount of money in those days. Yet in 1870 no fewer than 285 companies registered themselves in St Ives alone. Sadly, within fifty years this magnificent industry, its history and traditions spanning centuries, was dead.

The seining of pilchards was operated in the following way:

The first boat (the stop seiner), a low, broad and sharp-bowed vessel, measuring approximately 33 feet on the keel with a beam of 12 feet, was manned by six oarsmen and a cox and also carried the principal net, the stop seine. This was a net measuring 440 yards long, 33 yards deep in the middle, and tapering out to 24 yards deep at the extreme ends.

The second boat, of the same dimensions as the stop seine boat, was called the follower or, in East Cornwall, the 'volyer' (from its station of always 'following' the stop boat). The follower carried the tuck seine, a smaller net of approximately 160 yards long by 36 yards deep at the cod or middle. The follower also carried the stop seine capstan warps, and the grapnels and warps for mooring the seine.

A third boat called the lurker was a boat of 16–18 feet long which carried the Master Seiner, his assistant and two hardy boys. The purpose of the lurker was to provide a platform and advance post from which the Master Seiner and his attendants could wait and watch for the approach of fish and then direct the operation of shooting the seine.

In West Cornwall, particularly St Ives where because of the strength of the tides the nets had to be shot close inshore, the business of the lurker was performed from the cliff-tops by an experienced man locally referred to as the huer. Nicholas Ashton mentions the huers in his rare book of 1894 *Among Cornish Fisher Folk* and relates how, as the shoals neared the coast, they would call 'Hevva' through long tin trumpets to let the seiners know the fish were in sight. The rest of the operation of shooting and recovering the seine was directed by the huer using an elaborate set of semaphore signals.

The process of shooting the seine started as soon as the shoal was sighted. Firstly the huer or Master Seiner directed the stop seine boat in the operation of enclosing as much of, or all of, the shoal of pilchards within the stop seine. If needed, the volyer or follower may have been called up to complete the act of closing the gap in the stop seine. The shoal having been closed in was anchored and then towed, and finally warped by shore-based capstans, until the nets were in shallow enough water for the foot ropes to be firmly settled on the floor of the sea. Once the seine was in the sheltered, shallow water, the seines were made secure and the process of emptying or tucking the seine began. The great beauty of this method was that the fish could be kept in their net enclosure for several days, being removed at precisely the amount required for the process of balking in the pilchard palaces

When fish were sighted by huer, hevva was made by calling through the trumpet

Weigh anchor

Go to Eastward

Go out to Sea

Wind away warp, stop by dropping left hand.

See or Stand Quiet

'Get all ready' shouted through trumpet

'Cowl Rooz' or Cast net

Go to East

Go right Eastward

Steady

Go to Westward

Come together

Down anchor OR cancell all previous signals when there are no fish

THE METHOD OF SIGNALLING WITH BUSHES USED IN PILCHARD SEINE FISHERY ashore. This ensured that the fish were always in prime condition when they were piled into the balks for pressing.

The process of bulking or balking pilchards was done by first putting a heavy layer of salt on the floor of the fish cellar or palace, then on that a layer of fish, then a layer of salt, then a layer of fish and so on until the stack was five or six feet high, a catch of 200 hogsheads would take 24 hours to stack. After a month's salting the balk was broken into and the fish taken out and washed before being packed in barrels. The fish were laid in barrels by the fish maidens, tails toward the centre. The barrels then had a small lid called a buckler placed on the top. A large weight or stone was placed on the buckler and this, in the period of ten days, would press out the train oil, which would run away to drain into tanks for later sale. During the pressing process the barrels were periodically opened and topped up with more fish. Finally the barrel was back laid, so top and bottom looked alike. Each barrel contained about $4^{1}/_{2}$ cwt and held about 2,500 fish. Women were paid 2s. 6d for each barrel packed. Once packed, the barrels were exported to Spain, France and Italy. In 1811 a cargo sent out from Cornwall under licence was seized by the French and, through them, sold to the Italians for the enormous price of £9 per hogshead.

The Napoleonic Wars created great restrictions in the export of pilchards and for a time the traditional European markets virtually closed and new export markets were anxiously sought. There had already been a small export trade of pilchards to the West Indies, but the wars provided a great incentive to expand it even further. The West Indian market was thought to be capable of absorbing 180–200,000 barrels of pilchards per annum – an incredible number – to be used in the feeding of slaves on the sugar plantations. During this period large numbers of pilchards had been dumped or disposed of as manure, or even burnt. However, the West Indian market did present special problems: fish destined for the Indies required curing twice which, of course, meant using twice as much salt. The main obstacle was that the rum from the colonies, which was how the pilchards were to be paid for, barely covered the cost of conveyance.

The pilchard trade, however, was very valuable during this period. Its extent can be judged by a cooperage advert of the time, advertising a thousand 32-gallon barrels, well suited for the West Indian or other market. In 1815 peace returned to Europe and trade went back to its former markets, although attempts to continue the West Indies trade continued as late as 1830, with traders operating from Bristol.

CHAPTER NINE

FISHING NETS
— CONSTRUCTION AND CARE

Before the invention of synthetic fibres, nets were constructed from hemp, cotton and other natural fibres. Apart from regular mending and ransacking, nets needed soaking in preservative solutions. The earliest method was soaking in oak bark cutch. This was made by collecting oak bark, chopping it into small pieces, and boiling for many hours until the full strength had been steeped from the bark. The resulting solution, known as cutch, was used as a preservative as frequently as once a week. Nets could be seen in any seaside town and village hanging over the seafront rails, either drying before or after being cutched. In many of the larger ports special drying meadows and yards were a feature of the town. When cotton nets were introduced a special kind of cutch was used, called Burma or true cutch. This was derived from a shrub called Acacia Catechu (from which 'cutch' gets its name), grown in India and Burma. Cotton nets last much longer if kept in use – 'the wetter the better' was the rule of thumb for cotton nets.

Almost every village in Cornwall had some skill which set it apart from its neighbours and net-making was practised at Cadgwith, Looe, Mevagissey, Porthleven, St Ives, St Mawes, Mousehole and Newlyn. Some villages specialized in a particular kind of net. Cadgwith, for example, specialized in the construction of trammel nets. There were also many ways of setting up a drift net depending where it was to be used and what it was to be used for.

When nets were constructed of hemp, cotton and other natural fibres, the process of cutching always caused a great deal of shrinkage. This factor had always to be borne in mind when the net was being constructed. In West Cornwall the mackerel nets were often soaked in cutch then dried and then soaked again in a mixture of pure, clear coal tar with a little creosote added. The second process not only preserved the nets but had a softening effect on the fibres and made them easier to handle. Pilchard nets were soaked in a pickle made from creosote and green oil then wrung out and dried. This resulted in a very soft and flimsy net which had several other advantages: good preservation, little shrinkage and no breaking away at the knots. The disadvantages

Details of Construction of a Drift Net ~

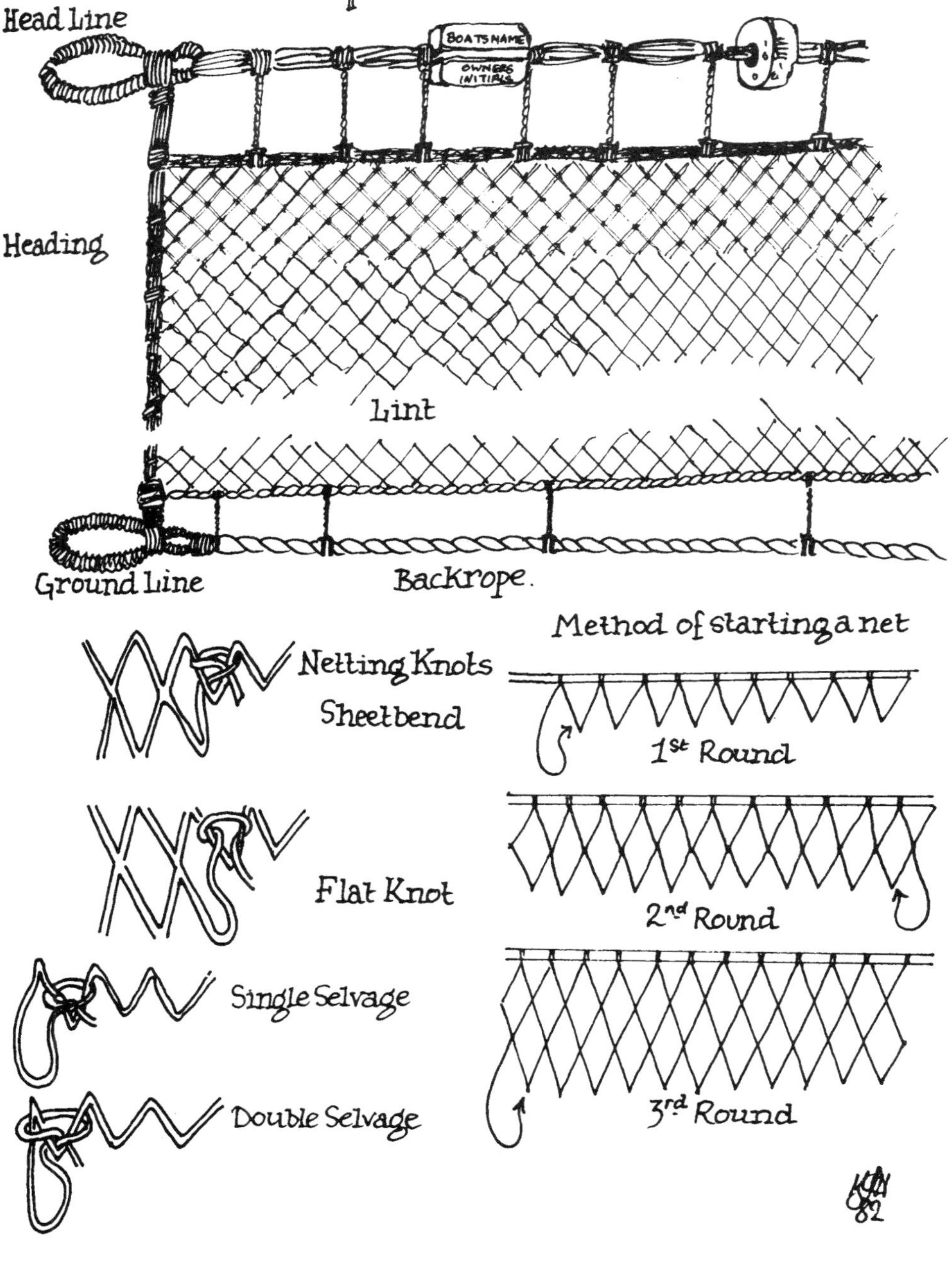

Head Line

BOATS NAME
OWNERS INITIALS

Heading

Lint

Ground Line

Backrope.

Netting Knots
Sheetbend

Flat Knot

Single Selvage

Double Selvage

Method of starting a net

1st Round

2nd Round

3rd Round

KJN
82

Methods of Setting up Drift Nets

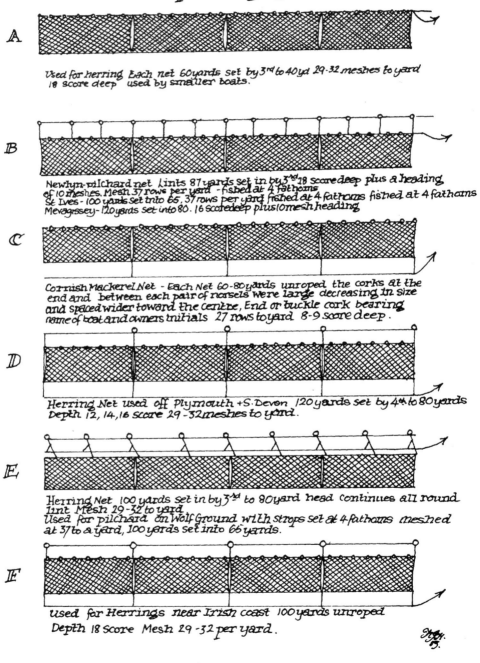

A

Used for herring Each net 60yards set by 3rd to 40yd 29-32 meshes to yard 18 score deep used by smaller boats.

B

Newlyn-pilchard net Lints 87 yards set in by 3rd 18 score deep plus a heading of 10 meshes. Mesh 37 rows per yard - fished at 4 fathoms
St Ives - 100 yards set into 65, 37 rows per yard fished at 4 fathoms fished at 4 fathoms
Mevagissey- 120 yards set into 80. 16 score deep plus 10 mesh heading

C

Cornish Mackerel Net - Each Net 60-80 yards unroped the corks at the end and between each pair of norsels were large decreasing in size and spaced wider toward the centre, End or buckle cork bearing name of boat and owners initials 27 rows to yard 8-9 score deep.

D

Herring Net used off Plymouth + S. Devon 120 yards set by 4th to 80 yards Depth 12, 14, 16 score 29-32 meshes to yard.

E

Herring Net 100 yards set in by 3rd to 80 yard head continues all round lint Mesh 29-32 to yard
Used for pilchard on Wolf Ground with strops set at 4 fathoms meshed at 37 to a yard, 100 yards set into 65 yards.

F

Used for Herrings near Irish coast 100 yards unroped
Depth 18 Score Mesh 29-32 per yard.

50

were that nets so treated took a long time to dry and tended to overheat in prolonged storage. Pickled nets were usually dipped at regular intervals throughout their lives. At Mevagissey these periodic dips were in a mixture of creosote and Stockholm tar, but every village and almost every skipper had his favourite method of preserving his nets, ropes and sails, and many exotic cocktails came into being.

The twentieth century saw the development of man-made fibres but these came too late for the luggers. The smell of cutch, creosote, tar and fish must have been as evocative of that era as the lure of steam and hot oil is to many latter-day steam railway enthusiasts.

The Luggers' nets were never the sole property of any one person. In the case of mackerel nets there were usually forty-five or so nets on board when the mackerel season commenced in January. These nets were owned in the following ratio: if the skipper also owned the lugger he would put 15–18 nets aboard, otherwise he and the owner would put 8–10 nets each aboard; the second, third, fourth and fifth crew members would then be expected to put 5–7 nets each aboard. As well as nets, each man had to buy a corresponding amount of footropes for his fleet and these were joined to the nets by ropes known as lanyards. In the 1890s nets cost, with head rope and corks but no foot rope, about £1. The foot rope cost a further 14s.

The villages and towns of Hayle, Fowey, Marazion and Newlyn all had rope-walks, so did Mousehole and Mevagissey and probably more besides. Cork for the construction of end marker buoys was sold at 12s per cwt. In 1914 the cost of a net was roughly equal to the market price of a cran (1,000 herrings), i.e. £2.10s. By the outbreak of the Second World War, when the prices really began to spiral, the same net would have cost £10, whilst a similar amount of fish would only have realized £4.10s.

Nets deteriorate for three main reasons and they are:
1   They may rot owing to the action of bacteria and/or mould when stowed in a damp condition.
2   They become weakened by mechanical wear and tear.
3   They may become weakened owing to heating induced by stowage in bulk when all decaying matter has not been removed from them. This may even result in spontaneous combustion.

The main agents used to prevent deterioration in natural fibre nets are:
1   Tanning materials such as are extracted from the barks and galls of oak trees; Burma or true cutch from the Acacia Catechu; Mangrove or Borneo cutch from the bark of mangrove trees.
2   Tar and tar products such as coal tar, Archangel and Stockholm tar.
3   Creosote, green oil, or pickle from tar distillation.

4 Linseed oil from crushed flax seeds.
5 Alum.
6 Cuprous compounds, copper oleate, copper napthanate.

Many inshore boats, such as gigs, used the trammel net as a method of catching a wide variety of fish for the market and also to provide bait for the crabbers. Many 'Covers' favoured the trammel net, often making their own nets or buying from makers at Cadgwith and Bridport. The prices quoted by Hounsell's of Bridport in their 1884 catalogue were:

10 fathoms long by 6 feet deep –	£1.10s
15 fathoms long by 6 feet deep –	£2.5s
20 fathoms long by 6 feet deep –	£3
25 fathoms long by 6 feet deep –	£3.15s
20 fathoms long by 9 feet deep –	£3.16s 8d
25 fathoms long by 9 feet deep –	£4.16s
20 fathoms long by 12 feet deep –	£4.10s
30 fathoms long by 12 feet deep –	£6.15s
50 fathoms long by 12 feet deep –	£11.5s

Barking could be done either by Hounsells or locally at a rate of 7 ½p per 10 fathoms of 6 feet deep pieces. The trammel net was used all around the coast and fishing was carried out in the following way:

Two buoy lines with corks or floats at intervals, and a weight or killick stone at the ends, weight about ½ cwt, were provided. To one rope, close to the stone or weight, the foot rope of the net and at the breadth of the net was made fast. Above the stone, the headline was made fast, taking care not to stretch the trammel up too high or else the strain would come on the net instead of the buoy line. The buoy line was placed carefully in a coil, with the stone, in the middle of the boat. The headline was placed in the starboard side of the stern sheets with the footline on the port side. As the crew worked back through head and footline, the trammel bunt would naturally fall between the two. When they reached the other end of the net the other stone and buoy were made fast. The marker buoy was thrown over the side and the sinker was lowered. Then the net was paid out.

A trammel was never shot with the tide against it or across it, as the latter pressed the net on to the sea bed and reduced its efficiency. Many fishermen only used one trammel, using a 40 fathom net if they were only after bait. If more nets were used they preferred joining up 30 fathom nets rather than carrying long spans. The reason for this was, if a net fouled the bottom and had to be torn out, damage could be limited to one span of net.

The trawl net was not used by the Cornish fishermen but by the East Coast fishermen and Plymouth and Brixham trawlers off the

Diagram Showing Construction of Trammel Net

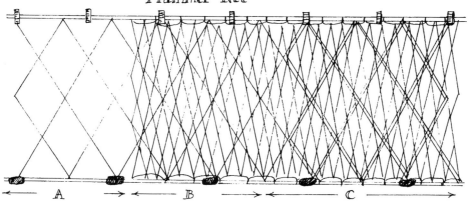

A - Far Armouring
B - Far Armouring & Lint
C   Far Armouring, Lint & Near Armouring

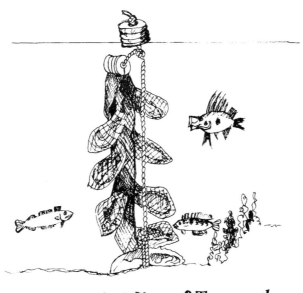

End View of Trammel

Shooting

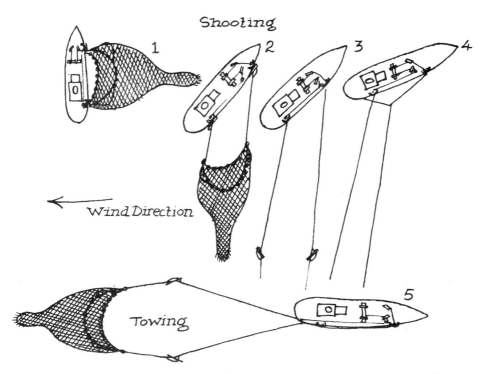

1   2   3   4

← Wind Direction

Towing

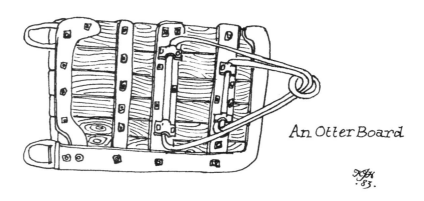

5

Stages 1-5 in Shooting an Otter Trawl.

An Otter Board

coasts of Cornwall, often to the annoyance and anger of local men. The trawl is a large, bag-shaped net which is dragged along the sea-bed by a boat. When the bottom is free of rocks and snags, it is used to catch a great number of prime fish, such as sole, plaice, turbot, cod, whiting, etc. Most trawls were and are made with pockets inside the body of the net. These are to entrap soles, which otherwise would swim quickly back out of the net. Some trawls have as many as six pockets made in them but ordinarily two suffice. There are two types of trawl; the beam trawl, which was favoured by the Brixham men, and the more modern otter trawl, which came into its own with the advent of the steam engine and internal combustion engine. The lug sail never lent itself to trawling, whereas the cutter rig with its large mainsail was ideally suited to the job. Beam trawls were towed by craft of various sizes.

The size of beam for a 20 foot boat would have been 12–14 feet whereas a vessel of 50–60 feet would have dragged a trawl with a 36–38 foot beam.

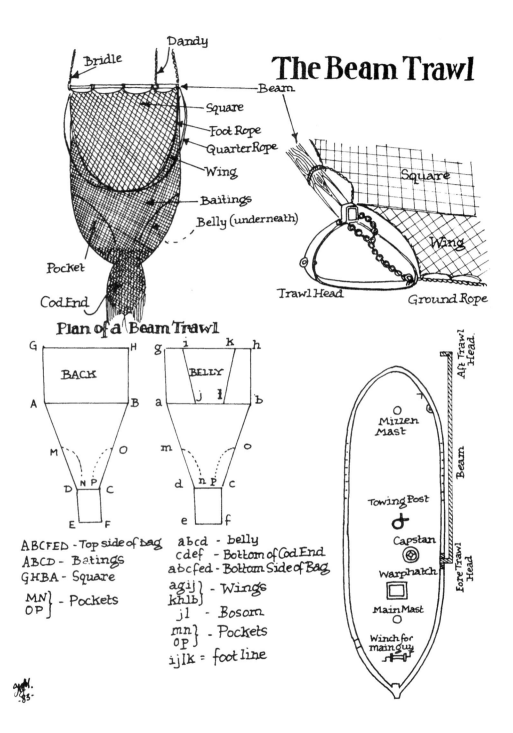

The Beam Trawl

Bridle

Dandy

Beam

Square

Foot Rope

Quarter Rope

Wing

Baitings

Belly (underneath)

Pocket

Cod End

Square

Wing

Trawl Head

Ground Rope

Plan of a Beam Trawl

G   H   g   i   K   h

BACK   BELLY

A   B   a   b

M   O   m   O

D N P C   d   n P   C

E   F   e   f

ABCFED - Top side of bag   abcd - belly
ABCD - Batings   cdef - Bottom of Cod End
GHBA - Square   abcfed - Bottom Side of Bag
MN }   agij }
OP } - Pockets   khlb } - Wings
                            jl - Bosom
                            mn }
                            OP } - Pockets
                            ijlk = foot line

Aft Trawl Head.

Mizzen Mast

Beam

Towing Post

Capstan

Fore Trawl Head

Warphatch

Main Mast

Winch for main guy

CHAPTER TEN

CRABS, LOBSTERS, CRAYFISH AND OTHER SHELLFISH

Pots have been used in Cornwall for the capture of all kinds of fish, from crabs, lobsters and crayfish to the taking of wrasse (presumably this was for the future baiting of lobster pots, wrasse being excellent bait for lobsters). Small pots made from fine withies were used in West Cornwall and the Scillies for wrasse. Nowadays pots made of polythene or plastic- covered steel come in two sizes and are mass-produced, but in the age of the lugger all pots were made from willow withies. Many areas of marshy ground were cultivated into withy gardens for this purpose. Pots were made in Portwrinkle, Fowey and Polruan, Mevagissey, Gorran Haven, Portloe, Porthscatho, St Mawes, St Just in Roseland, St Anthony, Coverack, Cadgwith, Mullion, Prussia Cove, Penzance, Mousehole, Penberth, Porthgwarra, Sennen, St Just in Penwith and Pendeen. Sennen even had a type of boat, which was unique to that cove, designed and used exclusively for the crab and lobster fishery. The Sennen Cove crabber was a sailing lugger with no accommodation. Its distinctive feature was 'hurrels' or cut-outs in the gunwhale through which the crews could row; when the oars were not in use the hurrels were blocked with wooden shutters.

At some places extra-large pots were made. Often measuring five feet in diameter, these pots were used to store successive catches, alive, until either a good number had been collected or until market prices had improved. In such places as Porthgwarra, special permanent stores were built into the crannies. At Port Isaac store pots were kept in specially constructed tidal pools which could be drained when the fish were required for packing.

The crab or lobster pots were strung together in strings of up to thirty, the pots being spaced according to the area they were being dropped so that only one pot needed hauling by hand at one time. The pots were then weighted with stones and, when in the chosen place, an anchor and marker dhan was bent on to both ends and the pots were baited and shot as the boat moved over its chosen ground.

Fresh bait such as ray bodies, mackerel, gurnard, pilchards or wrasse were used for crabs, whilst lobster and crayfish favoured bait of

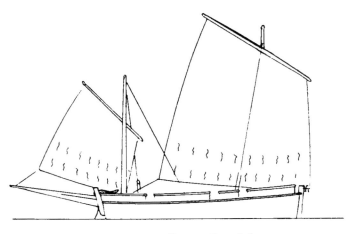

A Sennen Cove Crabber

an older or staler nature. The bait was secured to the pot with a small stake driven through the side of the pot through the bait and into the mouth of the pot. Before and after shooting the pots, care would be taken to ensure that landmarks were recorded so the exact location of the fleet of pots could be found again. The pots, once in position, would, if they continued to catch fish, remain in the same position for the whole season from May till December, only being lifted to be emptied and rebaited once or twice a day. They would also be lifted and moved to a sheltered spot if an early warning of bad weather and the ensuing ground-sea was obtained. If the pots were lost they could often be relocated by consulting shore-marks and dragging grapnels over the area.

In many of the older cottages and houses in Cornwall gardeners are often amazed by the large number of sea shells, particularly limpet shells, in the soil. 'Trigging' or gathering shellfish such as cockles, limpets and mussels is an old Shrove Tuesday custom in West Cornwall. In many parts of Cornwall 'Trig' meat supplemented the diet all year round. It never seems to have been conducted in an organized or commercial way but on an individual basis. With basic home-made tools, anyone could engage in a day's 'trig-picking'.

The other form of shell fishing which is carried on unchanged up to the present day is oyster fishing. From sailing or rowing boats, this was formerly carried out at Colchester, Whitstable, Burnham, Portsmouth, Saltash and Jersey, as well as on the Truro and Helford Rivers. Sadly only the fisheries on the Truro, Helford and Fal rivers remain. The Fal oyster beds became infected by a disease known as Bonamia in the early 1980s which resulted in the entire fishery being closed down between 1981 and 1984. Over the last decade the fishery has made a steady recovery. In recent years the Falmouth Oyster Festival in October has highlighted the unique flavour of the Falmouth oysters.

The fishery around the Fal has for many years been the last bastion of traditional sailing fishing boats with many of the boats in use dating back to the nineteenth century. *Victory, Winnie, George Glasson, Evelyn, Memento* and *Florence* were all built prior to 1900 and all are still afloat, many still working, and all credit to their skippers and owners. All of the above sailed in the 2009 Falmouth Working Boat World Championship, hosted at St Mawes. Every year on 5 November the oyster fishermen take the day off in celebration of a victory over foreshore rights won many years ago. The idea of a race for working boats on this date came from the Flag Officers and Commodore of the Mylor Yacht Club. The concept was to give the port's working boats an opportunity to race under their working rig: The boats race around a course over the local oyster-beds using the same gear and sails as they would on a normal day. 'The Silver Oyster Race', named after the trophies, silver-plated oysters mounted on wooden plinths (the inspiration of Peter Grigg, Commodore of Mylor Yacht Club), has proved to be a popular event in the Falmouth sailing calendar.

Cornish Crab ~ Lobster Pot.

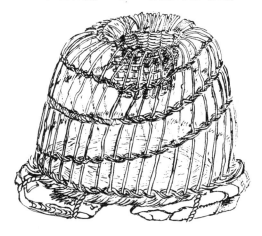

Cross Section of pot showing position and method of fixing Bait.

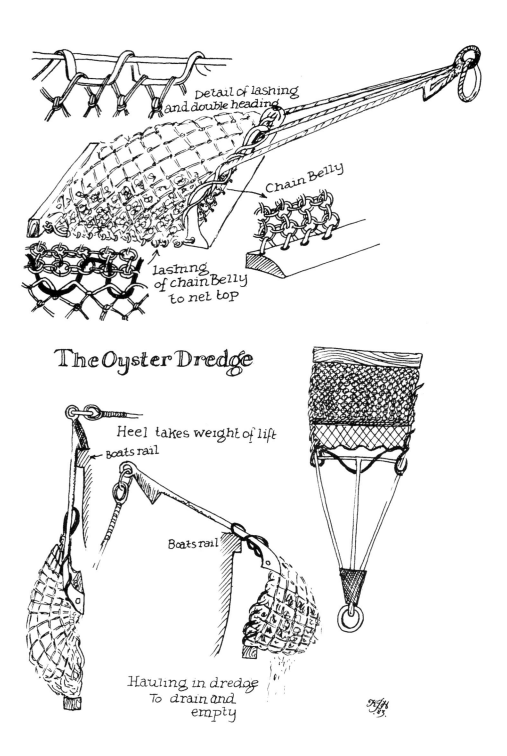

Detail of lashing
and double heading

Chain Belly

lashing
of chain Belly
to net top

The Oyster Dredge

Heel takes weight of lift

Boats rail

Boats rail

Hauling in dredge
To drain and
empty

Chapter eleven

Spear fishing

Spear fishing dates from antiquity and has probably existed since prehistoric times. Certainly the Egyptians, Romans and Greeks all used the spear or trident as a means of fishing. Poseidon (Neptune) the God of the sea is always depicted holding a trident or fish spear. Cornwall's sandy harbours and muddy estuaries were ideally suited to this type of fishing, whereas a rocky cove was not. A hard, stony sea-bed was not best calculated to preserve the sharp points of the spears.

There were three ways of fishing with a spear, one from a boat and the other from the riverbank, or wading in the water. If a boat was used, one of light draught was essential. If the fisherman was fishing on his own he would have provided sufficient ballast to counter-balance his own weight and, placed in the stern of the boat in this way, he would have been able to take his station in the bows of the boat and keep the boat on an even keel. The boat was then propelled by the fisherman using the spear as a paddle. If two men were in the boat they would obviously dispense with the taking on of extra ballast. The man in the stern would propel the boat with a spear and also take any fish that came his way whilst the bowman would watch for any fish scuttling away ahead and, after noticing where they had stopped to bury themselves, would, by the inclination of his spear, signal the man in the stern where he had to put the boat in order to get the fish.

If the fishing was done by wading, during the summer months, the fisherman would have probably used a spear very similar to the fluking pick. With this he would have repeatedly struck the bottom in the hope of impaling any fish lying in the sand.

Often a bucket, with a glass bottom was used to obtain a better view of the sea-bed. This was sometimes lashed to the bows of the punt with the bucket's base in the water. The fisherman could then have a clear view as the boat moved over the ground he was fishing. A great deal of practice is needed to fish with a spear because the refraction of light when it enters water causes the spear's shaft to appear bent. Allowance must be made not only for this but also for the magnifying effect of the water. Spear fishing is no longer carried out on a commercial basis in Cornwall but can sometimes be seen in operation on the Isles of Scilly where one or two individuals still use the spear in preference to the hook-and-line.

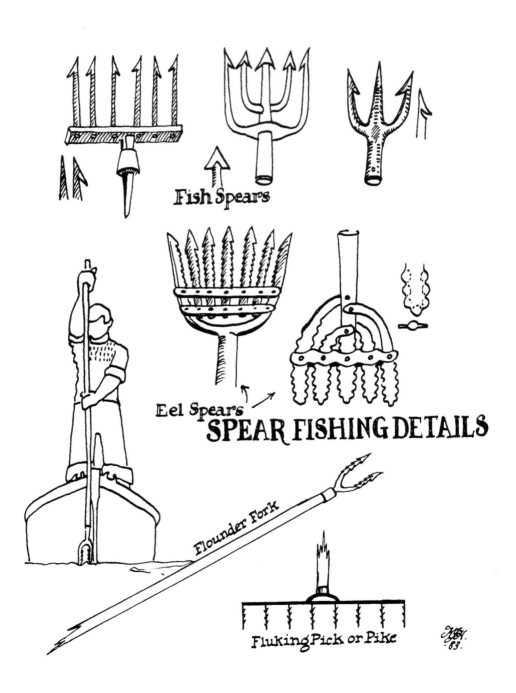

Fish Spears

Eel Spears

SPEAR FISHING DETAILS

Flounder Fork

Fluking Pick or Pike

CHAPTER TWELVE

THE TITHE SYSTEM

The tithe system was, in effect, a form of income tax levied by the Church of England at a rate of 10 per cent. On the land this tenth was extracted at harvest time and the proceeds of harvest tithes were collected by the local vicar and stored in a tithe barn, of which many still exist. In the Middle Ages or 'age of faith' as it is known, when the majority of the Church buildings were raised, the tithe was regarded as a necessary tax and was paid without resentment or malice. But with the growth of a more secular outlook opposition steadily increased and by the nineteenth century tithes had become a most unpopular and resented tax. This resentment was further increased in Cornwall by the fact that many sailors were Methodists and held no allegiance to the Church of England. Even those who did belong to the established Church weren't enamoured of the fact that many tithes fell into the hands of private landowners, and proceeds did not go for Church use at all.

The Cornish drift and line fishermen, who were, in the main, exceptionally poor, bitterly resented their tithe and gradually various places won exemption from paying. The seine owners, however, often well-to-do businessmen, could hardly plead poverty and the St Ives seiners, in particular, carried on paying the tithe until well into the 1880s.

The technical problem of collecting tithes on fish was a difficult enough business with willing contributors, but with hostile donors it became extremely difficult for a tithe owner to exact his dues. Consequently many County and High Court actions were brought before the Benches, and long and involved cases ensued. In at least one cove, and Sennen is a case in point, a toll was exacted on the use of a windlass or capstan used for hauling seines and boats back up the cove's slipway. However, this toll was held in much the same ill-favour as the tithe, and several court actions were brought by the owner of this toll, Lord Falmouth.

The most vociferous and ardent opponents of the tithe were the fishermen of Paul Parish. Their opposition spanned one and a half centuries from 1669, when one William Gwavas inherited Paul

Rectory and the tithe, right up until 1830 when, during the Christmas period a bailiff was sent to collect tithes. It was reported that the local fishermen deprived him of his pistols and the greater part of his coat, then pelted him with snowballs right up to the parish boundaries. Needless to say, no further attempts were made to collect the tithe and the fishermen celebrated their success by erecting, on the gable end of a cottage at the bottom of the slipway, which led from Street-an-nowan, a large board which read:

NO TITHE - ONE AND ALL

The board, complete with skull and cross-bone decoration, remained in position until the 1870s. This decisive action by Paul Parish's Newlyn 'buccas' amounted to a virtual coup de grâce for the tithe system in the Mount's Bay area. Elsewhere, the custom of tithes died out slowly and certainly did not survive the nineteenth century. A rebellious couplet of the time boasted:

We've cheated the Parson — we'll cheat him again
For why should we give him the one in ten!

CHAPTER THIRTEEN
Patmos
AND THE ARRIVAL OF STEAM

It has been said that when the early steam-driven ships first made their appearance off the coast of Cornwall, local fishermen and pilots would anxiously put to sea to assist what they thought was a ship on fire – only to find, on arrival, all well. The steamer, oblivious to the anticipation of the local crew's 'disaster', would cheerfully chug on its way.

The fisherman's conservative nature and general mistrust of the new, meant it was many years before steam propulsion was engaged for the purposes of fishing. In 1876 John Wedge from St Ives employed the famous engineering and shipbuilding talents of Harvey's, the Hayle-based shipbuilders and marine and mine engineers. They built for him a 43 ton, steam-powered, propeller-driven fishing vessel. The *Patmos*, as she was christened, had a very chequered career. She worked not only as a fishing vessel but was also used to carry general cargo, trading as far away as Rouen with sugar. Also the regular sailings of Harvey's own service to and from Bristol with their ship *Herald* were encroached upon by *Patmos*. This venture does not seem to have proved at all profitable and was abandoned, while *Patmos* returned to fishing.

Cornish boats had traditionally fished the Irish Sea and were used to friendly and hospitable treatment in Irish ports. So it was that the little steamer put into Dun Laoghaire, or Kingstown as it was then. The *Patmos* gave such a fine account of herself in the calm spell that followed, that the becalmed local fishermen attempted to set fire to her. This so unnerved her 'most inoffensive and respectable master' that he wisely left the place. Despite any and every effort to make the *Patmos* a money earner and despite her proven ability as a fishing vessel, working with drift nets and trawls, she was sold after two or three years, showing a net loss on her building price of £1,300 amounting to £500. From Cornwall she sailed for owners on the River Thames, but soon after this she was again sold and made the voyage to owners in South America.

An interesting half model of *Patmos* survives and may be seen in the museum at St Ives. The experiment with *Patmos* had a very sobering effect on further ventures and seven years passed before the *Willie*

Warren SS 31 was launched. Perhaps as a cautious decision, the *Willie Warren* was built as a paddle-propelled vessel rather than a screw-driven ship like the *Patmos*. Early expectations were again dashed when it was found her paddles were too small. Even when this was rectified her crew had great trouble, particularly if any sea was running, to ship and unship her paddles prior to fishing and returning home.

After much experimentation and, one imagines, much expense, the *Willie Warren* had her paddles removed and a propeller fitted. This also failed and the final transformation was to have the engines removed altogether and the boat re-rigged as a sailing dandy. Like her steam predecessor the *Patmos*, *Willie Warren* also sailed as a coastal freighter. Later it appears that new owners, possibly taking advantage of new technology, refitted her with a steam engine and renamed her *Rebecca*. Despite all the trials and tribulations of the two pioneer steam vessels, it does not seem to have put all owners off joining in the experiment and the St Ives registered *Edgar*, and the Penzance boats *Pioneer* and *Adventure*, are reported to have been very successful.

Perhaps the most imaginative and profitable use of steam by the West Cornish fishermen was formed when the Cornwall Railway forged a link with the lucrative markets in London. Unfortunately, like time and tide, the London-bound train from Penzance did not wait for any man and many luggers spent frustrating hours loaded with fish at sea in a flat calm whilst the time to the train's departure ticked away. To avoid this, all the catches or 'takes' were sent by fast boat to shore. This meant that only one boat at a time had to leave the fishing grounds and, of course, steam power, independent of a sailing breeze was ideal for the job. In April 1869, the Mount's Bay fleet employed the services of the paddle-steamer *Rover* and as many as forty boats took advantage of the service. Fish thus transported fetched high prices in the Billingsgate Market.

It was because of the initiative of the Hayle firm of Harvey and Co., that a regular steamer service between the Steam Packet Quay, Hayle; and Bristol was established. Harvey's original boat on the Bristol–Hayle run was, strangely enough, for owners with a flourishing shipbuilding yard, built in Greenock. The *Herald* was commanded by a great personal friend of Richard Trevithick. This choice of captain is not really surprising because Trevithick was a son-in-law of the owner of the ship. The *Herald*, under the captaincy of John Vivian, commenced service as early as September 1831 and was so efficient that it ultimately replaced the 'constant traders' link which had lasted for more than a hundred years.

The *Herald*'s success was such that a series of Harvey and Co. ships all sailed on the Bristol–Hayle, Hayle–Bristol run. The journey was done in 16–18 hours depending on a favourable tide, and cost £1.15s if one wished to have the use of a cabin, or 12s.6d if one braved the elements and remained on deck. A lady steward was in attendance in the Ladies' Cabin and 'refreshments of the best description, and at moderate prices', were provided on board. The *Herald* was later replaced by *Cornwall, Express* and *Cornubia*. A local firm, jealous of the trade and success generated by Harvey's service, launched first *Brilliant* and then *Queen*, but neither seems to have been quite as successful as the originator's vessels.

If fishing had been good, and the Mount's Bay fleet had landed the night before a Bristol Packet's sailing, all the horses and carts in the Penzance–Newlyn area were likely to be pressed into service to get the fish to Hayle and aboard the steamer before she left for Bristol. The road from Penzance to Hayle was reported to be just like a racecourse on such occasions with any number of vehicles on it, all trying to be the first in the dash for Hayle. 'I have known the *Cornwall*', said one contemporary, 'to be delayed for two hours after the proper time of sailing, taking the baskets of fish on board, whilst after all, there were always some men too late, who, with their steaming horses and carts of fish, were left lamenting on the quay, to curse their fate and sell their fish in the neighbourhood for what it would fetch.'

Another local occupation that benefited from Harvey's Steam Packets was that of farming, in particular the marketing of broccoli or cauliflower. This came about when the enterprising steward on the *Herald*, one Sharrock Dupen, bought a consignment of the vegetable when it was exceptionally cheap in Cornwall and sold it at great profit in Bristol and, in so doing, started a regular trade which was to develop into one of the most important branches of agriculture in Cornwall.

Chapter fourteen

Rhymes and sayings connected with the Cornish fisheries

Many rhymes used in forecasting the weather are common throughout the British Isles. Here are some that are or were peculiar to Cornwall:

Mist from the sea,
Brings fine weather to thee.
Mist from the hills,
Brings water for mills.

Rainbow to windward, foul fall the day,
Rainbow to leeward, damp runs away.

A sea mist was said to be:

All for heat an' pelchers (pilchards)

A fog and a small moon
Brings an easterly wind soon.

If the Lizard's clear,
Then rain is near.

Dr John Wolcot (1738–1819), who wrote under the pen name of Peter Pindar, penned many a poem or ode in praise of the pilchard and the Cornish ports from whence it was caught:

Pilchard! A thousand times as good as a herring.
Pilchard! The idol of a Popish nation,
Hail! Little instrument of vast salvation.
Pilchard, on which the Catholics in Lent are crammed,
Who, had they not, poor souls, this lively fish,
Would flesh eat and be consequently damned.
Pilchard! Whose bodies yield the fragrant oil
That makes the London lamps at midnight smile.

Peter Pindar's pen, but not his nose, thought the pilchard oil to be fragrant as another of his verses on the town of Mevagissey reveals:

Hail Mevagissey! With such wonders fraught
Where boats, and men, and trade and stinks are stirring
And Pilchards come in millions to be caught.

The subject of the pilchard is a recurring theme in many rhymes, odes and couplets. Often their authors' identities are lost to antiquity, as in this much-quoted example:

The Pilchards are come, and hevva is heard,
And the town from the top to the bottom is stirred.
Anxious faces are hurrying in every direction,
To take a fine shoal they have no objection.
The women now gathered before the White Hart,
Their hopes and their fears to each other impart,
"What Stem have you got?" "A first to the lea,"
"And look! Our men are now going to sea."
We see the huer with bushes in hand
Upon the White Rock he now takes his stand.
While "Right off," "Win tow boat," "Hurray" and "Cowl rooze"
Are signals no seiner will ever refuse.

The 'Stem' in the rhyme refers to the St Ives practice of allocating certain sections of the coast to certain seining companies. These sections or 'Stems', as they are known, were marked on the shore by a post or position between well-known landmarks. Boats were similarly distinctively marked so that it would be immediately obvious if a boat was fishing 'out of Stem'. The 'Stems' were named Carrack Lego or Cam Crowse, Porthnolver, Leigh, or 'Lea' as referred to in the poem, Porthmester or Porthminster, and Carrackgladen. Some sources say that the Stems were allocated rather as prizes after a regatta-like race, the first boat getting the first Stem and so on. This may have once been the case, but with two hundred and eighty-five seining companies registered in 1870 the more logical allocation of a position at the Stem was by a rota system. The signals which 'no seiner will ever refuse' refer to the semaphore-type signals which were made by the huer from his cliff-top position. These signals directed the seine boats into the best position to take as much of a shoal of pilchards as possible.

When launching the pilchard seine boats from Porthminster beach, children sang the following song:

A laky (leaky) ship with her anchor down,
Her anchor down, her anchor down,
A laky ship with her anchor down,
Hurrah, my boys, hurrah!

We're loaded with sugar and rum my boys,
And rum my boys, and rum my boys,
We're loaded with sugar and rum my boys.
Hurrah, my boys, hurrah!

I wonder if the 'sugar and rum' alludes to the pilchard-trade connection with the supplying of pilchards to the slave plantations of the West Indies during the early 1800s when the Napoleonic Wars had so disrupted the traditional European markets?

In Mousehole when a boat was launched from the builder's yard a man was engaged for a shilling wage to supervise and 'holla' or shout the rhythm for the men to haul the boat from the yard. His chant would go:

Alaw boat haul.
Alaw boat haul.
Haul.
Haul!

This would be to get the boat moving, as soon as the momentum had been attained, the chant would change to make sure the men had her in check, particularly on a slope. The supervisor would shout:

Stump and go!
Stump and go!

Until the tackles used in the launch had been drawn together or 'two blocks', the boat was then chocked, the tackles run or fleeted out, and the launch recommenced.

Of the many sayings associated with the pilchard fishery, none is better known than:

When the corn is in the shock,
Then the fish are on the rock.

Which refers to the fact that pilchards and harvest time usually coincided. After a successful pilchard season, each seining company would usually hold a dinner for all its employees. At these dinners the main toast of the evening was this oft-quoted rhyme:

Here's a health to the Pope,
And may he repent,
And lengthen by six months,
The term of his Lent.

For it's always declared
Betwixt the two Poles,
There's nothing like pilchards
for saving of souls.

ST. IVES SEIN BOAT BOW MARKINGS

Hocking Fish St.
Bolitho Western Cellar Island
Williams Fish St.
Hitchens St Andrews St.
Hitchens + Bazely Wharf Rd.

Bazely Wharf Rd.
Hitchens Wharf Rd.
Tremearne Fish St.
Tremearne Pudding Bag Lane
John Wharf Rd.

Best St Andrew St
J. Kernick
Brooking Williams Bunkers Hill
Union Co Rope Walk
J. Stevens Chy-an-Chy

Short & Dunn Copper Kettle
Independant Co North Place.
Edward Stevens Porthmeor Rd
Craze & Kernick
COLOUR CODES
Red
Blue
Yellow

Victoria Co Fish St
Rouncefield?
Matt Trewhella Norway Lane
Geo. Williams Norway Sq.
Ebenezer Co Fish St.

Batten Co Back Roads
John Tremearne Fish St. & Back Roads
James Williams Porthmeor
Cornwall Co Barnaloft Back Roads
Robt. Banfield North Place

S. Noall Wharf Rd.
Thomas T. John Bethesda Hill
Ross & Co.
Sherman Co Rope Walk
Tremearne Pudding Bag Lane

Best. St Andrews St
Jenkyn Fore St Digey Sq. Halsetown
Quick Commando Garage
Ebenezer Co. Porthmeor Rd.
J. Quick

71

Another colourful salutation referred to the profitable connection between Catholicism and the pilchard fishery. As one writer, tongue-in- cheek said, 'it enabled the Holy Father and his Catholic children to keep their Lent, by filling their bellies and fasting at the same time'. It was a common pre-season greeting:

Long life to the Pope,
Death to our best friends.
And may the streets run in blood.

The mackerel does not seem to have attracted the poetic attention of the County's rhymsters and poets. But this chant in the Cornish language was often called out as a kind of round amongst the crew of a mackerel lugger as the first nets were hauled:

Bryel; mata; tressa; peswera; pympes; wheffes
all scrawl along the line oh!

Bryel is Cornish for mackerel, the following five words are used to count, thus: a mate, a second, a third, a fourth, a fifth, a sixth and presumably 'all scrawl along the line oh!' indicated that after the sixth fish there were too many to count. Each crewman would shout one word in sequence. For one man or all to chant the whole rhyme would mean counting, and the counting of anything at sea was considered unlucky.

CHAPTER FIFTEEN

SUPERSTITIONS AND OMENS CONNECTED WITH THE CORNISH FISHERY. THE ST IVES SUNDAY FISHING CONTROVERSY

Bucca, apart from being a nickname used to describe a native of Newlyn, is also the Cornish name for an imp or hobgoblin. Fishermen, especially those from Newlyn, had a custom of leaving a fish on the beach or quay for Bucca. Sennen men would take a crust of bread to sea 'for luck', and miners underground frequently left a crust for Bucca as a talisman against disaster. Many objects of everyday life were – and still are by some – considered to be unlucky if mentioned at sea and when they had to be mentioned a substitute name would be used. For example, a priest or minister of religion, probably because they were against lucky, supernatural beings such as Bucca, was always referred to as a 'White Choker'. Church towers, often used in the taking of bearings at sea, were referred to as 'Cleeta'. 'Tower Cleeta', was a taboo name for St Buryan Church or, if in Mount's Bay, for Paul Church. 'Town Cleeta' was the taboo name for Cury Church.

Any animal, but particularly hares and rabbits, are never mentioned by name and rarely by taboo name, 'fur liners'. Any four-legged animal was usually dismissed in conversation as a 'two-decker' or 'four-legger'. Even the Wolf Rock was called by its old name, the Gulf.

At St Ives, the small people or coopers were said to tap the floors of houses before a large catch of pilchards and that the pressing stones in pilchard palaces would dance to foretell a large catch, was another belief. When pilchards were lying, stacked in bulk, they sometimes made strange squeaking noises as thousands of swim bladders simultaneously broke. This noise was referred to as 'crying for more' and was regarded as a good omen for the forthcoming fishery.

It has been suggested that a practice was followed of setting-sail model or miniature boats, or 'cok-dayba' as they were called, as a means of offering placations to sea spirits such as Bucca. Boats called 'cokyn baba' made of net corks, with a slate for a keel, were often sailed in Mevagissey and St Ives on Good Friday.

It has been recorded that, as recently as 1920, fishermen at Sennen would lock wives and daughters in the house to prevent them accidentally seeing shoals of fish before they had been safely netted. A universal bad-luck begetter was to whistle at sea or 'whistle up the wind' as it was called. Traditionally, the Cornish fishermen never worked on Sunday. In some ports, such as St Ives, where local boats still refrain from breaking the sabbath, there were strict laws against going to sea on a Sunday. A shoal of pilchards has been known to pass into St Ives Bay on a Sunday and because it was the sabbath, be completely ignored. Because of this dogged observance, the arrival of the East Coast men, who fished seven days a week, put a great strain on the friendly relationships many had built up with the 'Yorkies' while following the traditional summer fishery from Whitby and Scarborough. The Yorkies had no tradition of observing the sabbath, so when they started to catch, land and subsequently choke the markets and diminish the price of local fish, much ill feeling was generated.

In 1860 as a result of East Coast men landing and trying to sell 1,000 fish an altercation broke out between some St Ives fishermen, some strangers trying to buy fish, and the crew of the visiting boat. This resulted in the catch being consigned back to the sea. One thing led to another and, by May 1876, a large fleet of East Coast boats attempted to land fish. Such a commotion arose over the sale of these Sunday-caught fish that the Yorkies tried to take the fish to Hayle to sell them, but the local men were having none of that and a fight ensued. After an intervention, the Yorkies' fish eventually got away to Hayle, but the brooding resentment lingered on. The following year saw a repetition of the troubles and again the East Coasters were forced to Hayle. By 1877, the situation had spread to the Scillies and a chance encounter by rival crews sheltering at St Mary's led to a terrific riot which culminated in the Yorkie crews being locked up in the Garrison for their own protection. At the same time as the Scilly altercation, the St Ives men drew up conditions of sale that prohibited the sale of Sunday-caught fish and banned any purchaser of such fish from bidding at their sales. This resulted in the desertion of St Ives by all the East Coast boats in favour of Newlyn and was instrumental in the decline of St Ives as the major Cornish fishing port and the accession of the crown by Newlyn.

CHAPTER SIXTEEN
DISASTER
AND LOSS OF LIFE AT SEA

Fishing and mining have always been regarded as two of the most dangerous occupations entered into by man. Fishing on the coast of Cornwall with its massive granite buttresses, seas and winds running toward them for thousands of miles without let or hindrance, must be about the most dangerous.

On the north coast of Cornwall all the ports are tidal and a vessel having sailed a few hours before high water must return a few hours after or be forced to wait for the next tide. Whilst it would be possible for a 40 foot fishing boat to make a run around Land's End in all but the worst conditions and find shelter in Newlyn, small craft have no option other than to work the tides. When one considers a fleet of luggers fishing off the north coast of Cornwall miles 'up channel' with an ebbing tide and the prospect of a gale you could almost predict a wholesale disaster. Because of great skill and unsurpassed seamanship such a disaster never occurred. Which is not to say that accidents did not happen or boats founder, they did; but in the main the fleet would always return with crews, shaken, cold and wet, with tales to tell.

On 22 November 1872 the fleets of mackerel and pilchard drivers had left St Ives and were well offshore when the fresh to strong wind of the day began to increase to gale-force strength. The pilchard boats fishing locally hauled in their gear and made port safely. The mackerel fleet, however, was further off and had to beat into port. By 3 a.m. on the following day with the wind still blowing a gale, eight boats had still not been sighted. As the dawn rose, news of the eight filtered in. The *J.P.H.* was sighted two miles off St Ives Head, in a sorry state. The gale had torn away her mizzen-mast and sails and the exhausted crew had dropped anchor. Immediately the driver *Ebenezer* was manned and eventually got the crew of five safely back to port. Before noon the lugger *Boomerang*, true to her name, returned whence it had gone, bringing back an exhausted crew. The *New Susan* and *St Peter* eventually made Newquay with their sails in tatters. The *Daniel* had run for St Agnes. The crew of the *Ellen Noah* spent 24 hours riding to a raft (made up of spare sails and spars and steamed on the weather side of the boat to provide some respite from breaking seas). They

200 years of Small Sailing Vessels Wrecking Off The Coast Of Cornwall 1750~1950

Industry 1912   Emmanuel 1758
Pearl 1884   Joseph Ange 1753
Caroline 1792

True Blue 1860   St Marie 1914
Caroline 1867   Elizabeth 1808
Chere   1874   Mary Sprat 1891
Pearl   1825   Spartan 1846
Agenoria 1835   Engineer 1897
Jylt   1908   Judith
Jessie 1893   Hodbarrow Miner 1908
Lyme Packet 1824   Lord Duncan 1850
Friends 1874
Ocean   1832

Thomas 1852
Agnes 1845
Harmine 1871
Tagus 1838
Union 1866
Active 1830
Albert 1890
Irish Schooner 1836
Pendeen 1906

Mary Jane 1911
Brilliant 1841
Philomene 1920
Gleaner   1869
Chester 1854
Bessie 1912
New Jane 1854
Storm Nymph 1863
Forest Deer 1879
Heroine 1864
Emma Jane 1876

Lizzie Male 1877   Morwenna 1904   Brothers 1884
Renown 1913   Atlas 1829   Georges 1876
Young Eagle 1846   Appollo 1793   Flying Fish 1821
Expert 1894   Novator 1920   Lady Elliot 1864
Betsy 1794   Loftus 1862   Mary Elizabeth 1895
Comet 1852   Victoria 1862   Belmont 1920
Unity 1793   Immacolata 1875   Teazer 1901
Catherine 1852

Jane Ellen 1880   Anemone 1903
Douro 1872   Mary Peters 1923   Speedwell 1860
Ivy 1929   Constance 1865   Jane 1827   Brothers 1854
Bacchus   Emmelyne 1867   William + Anne 1854
Cecile Caroline 1880   Harmonie 1824   Jane 1886
Bona Fide 1930   Islander 1930   Lady of the Lake 1880
Sisters 1880   Jane 1838   Elizabeth 1891
Commerce 1871   Zarita St Pierre 1906
Rochellaise 1857
Katy Cluett 1917

Octavia 1921
Irene 1921
Richard Green 1887

Newmanly 1837   Sambre 1926   Emrys 1900
Venus 1849   Agnes 1911   St Leonard 1903
Southdown 1876
Starcross 1788
Ringdove 1829
Sarah Jane 1823
Princess Charlotte 1802
Puck 1874.
John & Rebbecca 1867
Aquilon 1891
Idea 1820
Violla 1922

eventually ended up at Ilfracombe. Sadly, two boats never returned. All that was ever found of John Paynter's boat *Mystery* was the midship section, some nets and gear and a mast bearing her registration number SS 411. Three sons of the owner and two other men had died. Of the other boat, *Captain Peter*, no trace was ever found, or of her crew of five. The storm's dreadful toll was two boats and ten men dead, leaving six wives and families without bread-winners. Every port has its own tale of disaster to tell.

In 1948 on the night of 25 June the Porthleven fishing boat *Energetic* PZ 114 crewed by six Richards brothers was out on a fishing trip, with them was a visitor friend, Roy Mewten. All was going well on board the little *Energetic* when suddenly, in darkness and fog, they were run down by an American steamer, the 7,218 ton ship *Chrysanthy Star*. In the words of a local paper '*Chrysanthy Star* suddenly loomed out of the thick fog and ran right over the little *Energetic* cutting her in half; she sank in seconds', taking with her, brothers John Henry, Billy, Perkin, Tom and Gilbert. One brother, Ralph, and Roy Mewten were rescued by the *Chrysanthy Star* but Mr Mewten died before reaching land. The tragedy of the *Energetic* occurred ironically on the eve of the annual festival of St Peterstide and is still remembered, vividly by some residents of Porthleven.

The coast between Land's End and Newlyn, normally an idyllic stretch of coast, has more than earned its title 'the fishing boats graveyard'. Its gory toll of wreck and disaster includes:

Unity, sank without loss of life off Lamorna, 1893
Arethusa, lost with all hands off Mousehole Island, 22 January 1895
Emmeline and Jonadab dragged anchors onto Island, April 1899
Excellent, Lowestoft steam drifter struck Bucks, May 1899
Vanguard, run down by Lowestoft drifter off Bucks, April 1904
Orlando, lost towing dismasted *Emblem,* October 1907
Emblem, lost on Hotel rock Mousehole, April 1914
Kia Ora, lost at Lamorna, 1920
Harry, Brixham sailing trawler lost Porthcurno, 1926
Young Charlie, struck the Bucks and sank off Penzer Point, 1926
Vierge Marie, Belgian trawler ran aground Tater Du, 1937
Vert Prairial, lost with seventeen hands at Wireless Point, 1956
Nazarene, ran ashore at Pedn-e-Vounder, 1957
Pluie De Roses, eighteen month old French crabber, hit cliffs at
  Porthcurno, 1959
Boy David, seventy ton trawler owned by Stevensons of Newlyn, hit
  Bucks and sank, 1961
Juan Ferrer, coaster whose loss at Cam Boscawen led to the building
  of the Tater Du lighthouse, 1963

Even the tragedy that befalls the Ancient Mariner in Samuel Taylor Coleridge's poem palls into insignificance beside the mythological act committed by the young fisherman of Padstow, who according to legend, shot with his bow not a 'soyle' or seal, as he claimed, but instead, mortally wounded a mermaid. She in turn, with her dying breath cursed the fisherman and his port and caused a bar of sand to rise up across the mouth of the river.

The town was Padstow and the Bar was the legendary Doom Bar, an aptly named spit of shallow ground that almost seals Padstow's estuary. Over the past century and a half the Doom Bar with its constantly shifting sands covering approximately a square mile, has claimed the lives of about one hundred and fifty mariners, about double that amount of ships of all sizes and three lifeboats.

Not all ships and fishing boats founder close inshore, however, as in the case of the *Desire* of Porthleven, skippered by Captain John Strike. She was run down by the 1,700 ton ship *Corlic* on 10 March 1871 and cut so completely in half that the Lowestoft boat *Happy Return* could sail between both halves. They found no survivors, but the teenage son of the skipper, Thomas Alfred Strike, had managed, despite a broken leg, to hang on to a trailing rope and had climbed aboard the vessel that had cut the *Desire* in two. Two Porthleven boats the *Wonder* and the *Mary Jane* later put to sea and towed the wreckage into Porthleven harbour. In the bow part a watch was found, stopped at 4.45 a.m. the precise time the *Corhic* had hit *Desire* and claimed the lives of seven of the crew. Thomas Alfred Strike was taken on the *Corhic* to Liverpool. After spending several months in hospital he returned to Porthleven where he eventually died aged 87.

On 7 October 1880, a tremendous gale saw the Mousehole lugger *Jane* and all her crew, dashed to pieces within sight of the harbour entrance at Penzance. The assembled crowd of horrified onlookers were helpless spectators of the tragedy. Many boats in this gale, though at their moorings, sank. Eight or nine sank in Newlyn, a further eleven sank in Mousehole. But the loss as great as the boats was the loss of nets and footlines left on the harbour wall to dry.

In 1882 in St Ives the fleet was riding to its nets when, without any warning, a north-westerly wind of hurricane strength got up and carried away almost every net. The total loss was estimated at £5,000, but the men, many of whom lived a hand-to-mouth existence, were rendered destitute. The men, thinking philosophically that they were lucky to escape with their boats and lives, encountered another gale on reaching home two days later. It was only through the seamanship of the crews, that the luggers *Theodore, Express* and *Hopeful* made port. The *Grace Darling* and another boat were not so fortunate and, after weathering a hurricane, both were sadly lost without loss of life in a mere gale!

In 1892 the St Ives lugger *Gideon* was driving to her nets fifteen miles west-by-north of Gurnards Head under a moderate east-north-easterly wind, when suddenly and silently, the schooner *Earnest* of Preston came up on her and drove straight through her. In 1909 the lugger *Family* suffered a similar fate when she was hit by the French steamer *Orne*. In 1879, while taking part in the summer herring fishery in the North Sea, the *Primitive* of Mousehole, fishing from Scarborough, was sunk in collision with a Dutch steamer *Talisman* eight miles out of Robin Hood's Bay. The following day on 9 September, the eighteen ton Penzance lugger *Malakoff* was sunk in almost the same spot after being hit by the *S.S. Erith* of London.

What price the cost of the free harvest?

Chapter Seventeen
FAMOUS VOYAGES
BY CORNISH FISHING BOATS

Of all the famous voyages made in fishing boats that of the *Mystery*, a half-decked lugger, which in 1854–5 sailed from Penzance to Melbourne, Australia, is one of the most remarkable. Probably the best version of the voyage is that given by one of the crew of seven, P. C. Matthews, in 1874, in order to set straight a garbled version of the voyage printed in a Penzance newspaper:

> *We left Mount's Bay on the morning of the 18th November 1854 with a crew of seven men Richard Nicholls, Job Kelynack, Richard Badcock, William Badcock, Lewis Lewis, Charles Boase and myself. Our cargo consisted principally of provisions and water. On 14th March 1855, we cast anchor in Hobson's Bay, Melbourne, thus accomplishing the voyage in 115 days, including seven days stoppage at the Cape of Good Hope, where we put in for a supply of water. We were 8 days from England to Madeira, and on the 35th day out we made the Island of Trinidad. On the morning of the 17th January 1855, we arrived at the Cape of Good Hope, being 59 days out. On January 24th at 6p.m. we got under way from Cape Town and proceeded on our way with H. M. Mails on board. Nothing interfered with our progress until February 18th in Lat. 40.5 south, Long. 82.5 East, where we encountered a very heavy gale which necessitated our riding to a raft for nine or ten hours. Riding hove-to under such circumstances. On February 23rd another heavy gale visited us in Lat. 39.57 south, Long. 98 East. We again rode to a raft for four or five hours. On 5th March, we met with another heavy gale in Lat. 40 South, Long. 129.19 East, which compelled us to ride to a raft for 12–14 hours. The weather was pretty favourable after that date until we got to our destination.*

The voyage was made in a boat measuring 33 feet long by 11 feet 6 inches beam and carrying navigational equipment no more sophisticated than a compass, an hourglass, the relevant charts, and a traverse board (a board, or commonly the bellows for the cabin stove, marked like the compass rose). The thirty-two points were marked on the board with the lines radiating from the centre, each with eight holes into which pegs could be inserted to mark how many half hours the lugger had sailed on a particular course. Equidistantly spaced, below the compass rose, were short vertical lines numbered one to twelve with four holes each. These were to record the speed for any hour of the watch. At the extreme right of these holes were three more vertical lines with four holes, each marked $^3/_4$, $^1/_2$, $^1/_4$, to enable fractions of a knot to be recorded. The pegs were secured to the board with string.

In 1937 as a result of a current Housing Act, the Local Council made a clearance order on a number of houses and fishermen's cottages on the Newlyn waterfront. The Penzance Council, taking advantage of the Act, had come to the decision that the properties in question were slums and that they should be demolished. The inhabitants were to be rehoused at their own expense on a nearby council housing estate at Gwavas, near the top of Paul hill in the Penwith area. Although in a motor vehicle the hill is no great problem, the thought of having to walk from the Newlyn Quay to Gwavas after a night's fishing, and having to come back down to land fish for the 8 a.m. market, only to re-climb it later in the day, must have been a very daunting prospect. Gwavas, unlike the quay-side houses, had no net-drying or mending facilities, nor did it command a view of the harbour, so a vessel in difficulties at her mooring in winter gales could not easily be supervised. Added to this, many of the men involved held the freehold of their cottage and were being asked to bear the cost of having it demolished, whilst all they were being offered was a council house which they were expected to pay rent for. After many futile local protests it was decided to take a fishermen's delegation to protest in London. A petition was drawn up:

We, the undersigned inhabitants of Newlyn and District, wish to protest respectfully and strongly against the wholesale destruction of our village. This ruthless appropriation of private property involves, in most cases, the loss of a lifetime's savings and the means of a livelihood. We claim that no such drastic action has been permitted in any other part of the country. We earnestly beg your very serious consideration of this disaster with which we are confronted.

So it was that on 20 October 1937 after her crew of nine had been to chapel in Boase Street, and to cheers and strains of *Fight the good fight* ringing in their ears, Captain Cecil Richards led his crew aboard the *Rosebud* and commenced their 460 mile voyage to Westminster pier. In London the *Rosebud* and her crew received a great welcome, Captain Alec Beechman, M.P. for St Ives, was among the welcoming party at the pier steps. Later they met Sir Kingsley Wood at the Ministry of Health. Sir Kingsley gave *Rosebud's* crew a warm welcome and promised to look at the petition and investigate the matter. *Rosebud*

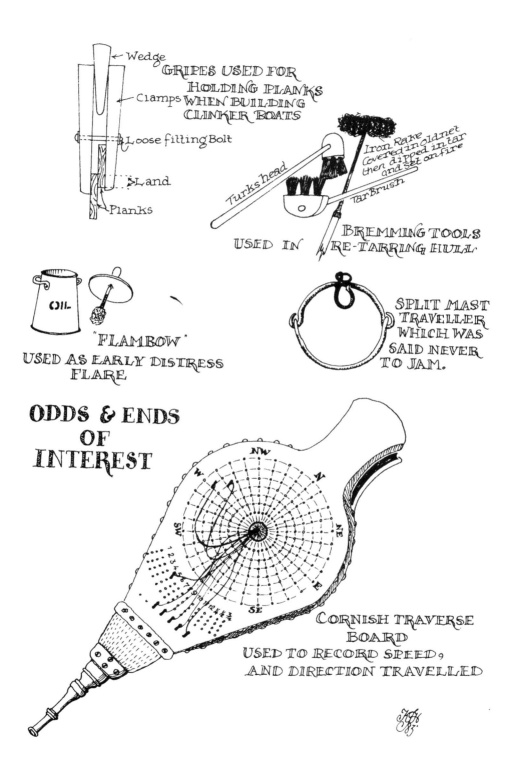

← Wedge

GRIPES USED FOR HOLDING PLANKS WHEN BUILDING CLINKER BOATS

Clamps

Loose fitting Bolt

Land

Planks

Turks head

Iron Rake Covered in old net then dipped in tar and set on fire

Tar Brush

BREMMING TOOLS USED IN RE-TARRING HULL

OIL

"FLAMBOW" USED AS EARLY DISTRESS FLARE

SPLIT MAST TRAVELLER WHICH WAS SAID NEVER TO JAM.

ODDS & ENDS OF INTEREST

CORNISH TRAVERSE BOARD USED TO RECORD SPEED, AND DIRECTION TRAVELLED became a celebrity during her stay and many Londoners, sympathetic to the men's cause, came aboard at a cost of 6d and made a wish on a bottle of Madron Well water and another from the River Jordan.

On the same day as the *Rosebud* arrived in London, a party of the wives of the crew, and Hilda Richards the skipper's daughter, representing the youth of Newlyn, left Penzance with another petition which they presented to the Queen. Their arrival in London attracted as much publicity as that of the fishing boat. The action of the *Rosebud*'s crew and that of their womenfolk was only partially successful. Of the one hundred and fifty-seven properties involved, only twenty-three received a total reprieve, fifty-four were purchased at their market value. Of the remainder, payments were made to seventeen, as being well-maintained houses. One block was deemed to be irreparable and was demolished, but facades were kept so as not to totally spoil the character of the waterfront area. Subsequently *Rosebud*, her moment of fame and glory over, went back to her trade. She later changed hands several times and was re-named *Cynthia Yvonne*. Under this name she lived out her last working days operating from Hayle in the 1970s. She was later hulked and left to rot away in in the sands of Lelant. The last bits and pieces of the *Rosebud* were hauled onto the old Dynamite Quay at Lelant in the late 1990s and a notice invited anyone who wanted a piece of the wreckage as a souvenir to help themselves. Within a short time the last vestiges of the *Rosebud* dissapeared, taken by souvenir hunters or simply those wanting some free firewood.

CHAPTER EIGHTEEN

POEMS ABOUT FISHING

The Fisher's Widow

The boats go out and the boats come in
Under the wintry sky.
And the rain and foam are white in the wind
And the white gulls cry.

She sees the sea when the wind is wild
Swept by the windy rain,
And her hearts a-weary of sea and land
As the long days wane.

She sees the torn sails fly in the foam
Broad on the skyline grey,
And the boats go out and the boats come in
But there's one away.

ARTHUR SYMONS
Poems

The Old Fisherman's Lament

Tis well an' fine for the steam trawler
 to sweep the floor of the say,
But turble hard for the fisherman
 as only sails the bay.
For the fish gets scaircer and scaircer
 an' hardly ait at all.
And what's to be catched with the
 seinin be barely with the haul.

We used to count on herrin's
 to buy us Chris'mus cheer,
But the catch runs lighter an lighter
 an' pervisions be allays dear.
An' what us gets in the crab pots
 that don't take long to sell,

Especial when most of the pots be gone
  on a long ground swell.

Tis a whish't poor life for a lad to lead
  an' mos'ly they won't abide,
But sterry away to the furrin ports
  athurt a keenly tide,
An' us be left, all lone and long to moil
  as best we may.
While the clanking trawler steams along
  an sweeps the floor of the say.

BERNARD MOORE, 1914

Verses on the curing of pilchards attributed to John Boson of Newlyn circa. 1700:

Hern (pilchard)

Yma ow han vy war hem, gans cok ha ros
My song is on pilchards, with boat and net
Kemerys in 'Sans' Carrek Los y'n Cos.
Taken in the Bay of St Michael's Mount.

Pan yu an cucow devedys tre
When the boats have come home
Dyworth mor, tus-porth 'Dega! Dega! a gry,
From sea, the haveners cry 'Tithe Tithe!'
Ha kenyver venen ogas a-den
And every woman draws near
Gans cowel ha try hans hem war hy heyn
With a cowl and three hundred pilchards on her back
Dhe wul barcados yn kenyver chy
o make bulks in every house
Gans garmer 'Lyes Hem Hem! Holan moy!'
With cries of 'Lots of pilchards, pilchards, more salt!'
Pan yns sallys da, un mys warbath
When they are well salted for one month together
Prys yma dhe squatta yn-ban ha tenna yn kerth
Its time to break them up and draw them away.
Wosa henna aga golghy glaneth yn dowr sal
After that, to wash them clean in salt water.
Y-fryn ry hannow da dhe'n mowsy-oll
It will give a good name to all the girls
Aga gorra splan y'n balyer, pen-ha-tyn
To put them bright into the barrel, head to tail.
Gober ha tra vras yns rag an varchons fyn.
They are a profit and a large concern to the keen traders.

Myreugh – why gwedhen, hyr tredhek tros,
Look for a pole thirteen feet long
Gorreugh war honna meyn a bymp cans-pos
Put upon that pressing stones of five hundredweight.
Try the myn y'n jeth, myreugh – why dhedha
Three times in the day look to them
Rag hanter mys dyworta saym a-vyn codha
For half a month train oil will fall from them
Yth-yu homma an forth wyr an hem dhe bara
This is the true way to prepare the pilchards
Y'n varghas wella y a-vyn gwertha.
In the best market they will sell.

Bledhen war vledhen gwra gorholyon dos
Year upon year may ships come
Ha gans hem lun dyworth Dowr Gwavas mos
And loaded with pilchards go from Gwavas Lake.
Worteweth gwra gwyns North Yst aga wetha pell
Finally may a north-east wind blow them far
Rag an bobel pow tom dh'aga dybry oll
For the hot country people to eat them all.
Yma peth hem kepar oll a'n bys
Pilchards are wealth alike of all the world
Mom a bobel voghosek es a bobel vras.
More of poor folk than of great folk.

Chapter nineteen

Fish and fishing on the Cornish coast

Fish and fishing on the Cornish coast. The fish, where to find them and the gear used in catching them.

Whiting *Merlangius merlangus.*
There are three fish caught under this general name: The Common or Silver Whiting, the Whiting Pollack and lastly the Coalfish or Sillock — this was known in Cornwall as the Race, or Rauning Pollack (an old Cornish word for ravening or ravenous), and is of a much darker colour green on the back and of a rounder form of body generally than the preceding classes.

Common or Silver Whiting *(Merlangius merlangus)*:
Found where the bottom is sufficiently soft and oozy to support the worms on which it feeds. It sometimes attains a weight of 4–5lbs but the most commonly caught fish will not exceed 2lbs. The early summer fish are almost always smaller than those caught later in the year.

Whiting are usually found in the 28–32 fathom range and between 2 $^1/_2$ and 6 miles from the shore.

Pollack or Whiting Cole or Coal *(Pollachius pollachius)*:
Although similar in shape to the Whiting, the Pollack is a different colour, being an olive brown on the back, the sides shading away to a yellowish white. It attains a much greater size, and fish of 15–20lbs are not uncommon. It differs quite as much in its habits as in its colour from the Whiting. The Whiting prefers the soft bottom, whereas the Pollack frequents the rocky ground particularly where rocks run a long distance to seaward, over which the tide sets strongly. They are more or less to be found at all seasons of the year wherever an extent of sunken rocks exists at a distance from the shore, as, for instance, the Eddystone off Plymouth, etc. They occasionally, however, disperse in pursuit of the sand eels or Launce and, after remaining for any length of time on the sandy bottom they become of a much lighter colour and improve in quality for the table, so that any fish over the weight of 6 lbs nearly equals Cod in firmness and flavour.

The best fishing for Pollack is on the S.W. Coast from March–July

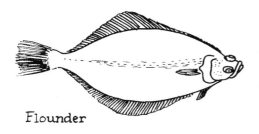

Flounder

CORNISH NAMES :- MEHAL MEHIL

Grey Mullet.

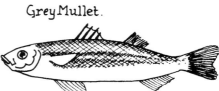

CORNISH NAMES :-
CUCKOLD, ELLICK,
GURNICK, RUDELLICK,
PENGARN, SODGER
REDFISH
TUBBY

Gurnard

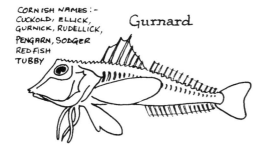

Haddock

CORNISH NAMES :- DYNSAK , TINSACK, HEEAK

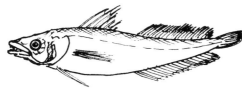

Hake

Herring

John Dory
CORNISH NAMES
JAN DORY.

Lemon Sole

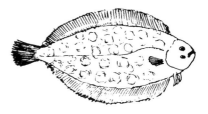

and in the deep-water reefs right up till Christmas. The Pollack feeds at all depths but much more above than on the bottom.

COAL FISH *(Pollachius virens)*:

Known in Cornwall as the Race or Rauning Pollack. The back is usually dark green but may be blue. The lateral line and belly are white. The Coalfish attains a larger size than the Pollack (up to 30lbs) but the flesh is inferior. It inhabits similar ground to the Pollack. Large fish keep to the outside of headlands with strong tidal streams, and they have sometimes been taken from the drift Herring boats with hook and line, mingled with Cod.

WHITING POUT *(Trisopterus luscus)*:

Whiting Pout, Rock Whiting, Short Whiting, Lady Whiting, Blinds, Bib and Blarns – all names for the 'universal' pout. It is one of the most common fish, both on mixed and rough ground, and it makes very good eating if cleaned immediately after being caught.

POWER OR POOR COD *(Trisopterus minutus)*:

Among the pouts, the 'Poor' (as it is known in Cornwall, or the Gilligant or Whiteyes in the North of the country) is the smallest of the Cod family. Usually taken when fishing for Whiting Pout. It must be eaten as soon as possible after being caught, as 24 hours out of water will leave it – although still fresh – quite tasteless. Caught from July to Christmas they rarely exceed 5–10 inches in length. They make good bait for conger.

DAB *(Limanda limanda)*:

The Dab is a first-rate fish when in perfect condition, which is in the early Spring. The Dab is often confounded with the flounder or fluke (Platessa flesus), as it is similar in size and shape. The Dab is rough on the back and nearly transparent whilst the flounder is smooth and opaque. When first caught, the fish is a delicate brown with mottles of crescent- shaped spots of bright orange, but these hues fade soon after being caught. They are found on all the sandy and oozy shores of the Cornish coast, both with the trawl-net and hook-and-line.

FLOUNDER OR FLUKE *(Platichthys flesus)*:

The Flounder or Fluke frequents large tidal rivers, and although evidently a sea-fish, will wander far into perfectly fresh water, and there live and thrive. The Flounder is very similar in shape to the Dab but inferior in quality; yet in the winter until the beginning of spring it is quite firm and, at this time of season when full of spawn, is quite palatable.

CORNISH NAMES :- LENESOW, MAIDEN (Youngling) RAUNING LING (Spent Ling)

CORNISH NAMES :- BRE'AL

Ling

Mackerel

CORNISH NAMES :-
  LANTERN,
MARY SOLE, MERRY SOLE,

Megrim

Pilchard

CORNISH NAMES :—
  HERN, HERNEN,

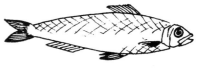

CORNISH NAMES :-
PLAETH

CORNISH NAMES :- AGA REVER, DUGAL, DIDGEL,

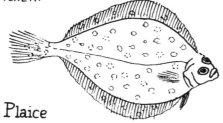

Plaice

Pollack

CORNISH NAMES :- BIB, DAMA GOTH, OLD WOMAN,
    BLIND, LAGATTA, BLENS,
    BOTHAK

CORNISH NAMES :-
  KARLATH

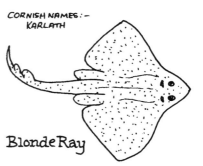

Pouting

Blonde Ray

MACKEREL *(Scomber scombrus)*:

This well-known fish, with its distinctive markings, was taken with both seine and drift-nets and the hook. The fish are taken at all times of the year, but the best fishing is to be had in July and August. The taking of winter Mackerel with the purse seine is a twentieth century development.

SCAD OR HORSE MACKEREL *(Trachurus trachurus)*:

This, although of the Mackerel family, is a coarse fish and consequently not held in much estimation. The lateral line of the fish is curved and marked with a succession of pointed scales, besides two spines close to the anal fin, which is as well to remember when unhooking them. As a bait, especially for prawn pots, they are useful. The fish was often salted down for winter provisions in Cornwall and the Scilly Isles.

BASS *(Dicentrarchus labrax)*:

The Bass, although a member of the Perch family, was often called the Salmon Bass because of its passing resemblance to the salmon. It forms large shoals in the mouths of rivers and estuaries, and can attain a weight of 15lbs and more. The fish generally appear on the surface of the water at the end of April or beginning of May, and may be caught fly fishing, ground fishing with baited hooks, or with the drift-net shot from the beach. Bass feed best in rough weather and disturbed water, and will approach the shore when the waves are breaking six or seven feet high.

DORY *(Zeus faber)*:

The Dory, or John Dory, is one of the most grotesque, and at the same time one of the best fish afforded by our seas. Head very large and very ugly, body deep and compressed, colour olive-brown with a golden yellowish tinge, a deep notch in front of the eyes, a black spot behind each gill cover, mouth capable of great protrusion, and head having a lantern-jawed appearance. It is very sluggish in its movements, floating or drifting along with the tide, but can exert itself when its prey is in sight. The Dory is taken amongst other fish in the trawl, seine, or trammel-net. One method formerly used by West Country fishermen, was to tie a small bream by the tail, without a hook, and the Dory on gorging it, the dorsal and pectoral fins stuck across the throat and did the work of a hook. The Dory emits a grunt when taken out of the water.

GREY MULLET *(Mugil cephalus)*:

This, although a sea-fish, can and does frequent brackish water and is perhaps of all sea fish the most capricious in taking the hook. Large quantities are to be met within the various docks and about piers and

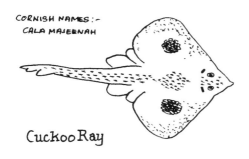

CORNISH NAMES :-
CALA MAJEENAH

Cuckoo Ray

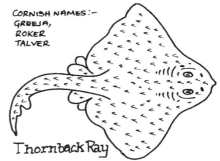

CORNISH NAMES :-
GREEJA,
ROKER
TALVER

Thornback Ray

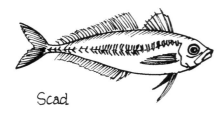

CORNISH NAMES :- HORSE MACKEREL

Scad

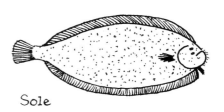

Sole

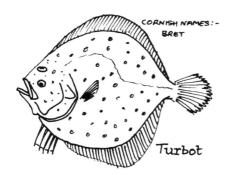

CORNISH NAMES :-
BRET

Turbot

CORNISH NAMES :- BAWD . BULL WRA, GUCKOO
JACKY RALPH, JOHN RAA,
RASP, WRAH

Ballan Wrasse

CORNISH NAMES :- BUCKHORN (When dried)
GWIDNAK
SCALPIONS (When dried)

Whiting

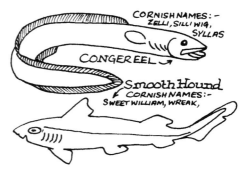

CORNISH NAMES :-
ZELLI, SILLI WIG,
SYLLAS

CONGER EEL

Smooth Hound
CORNISH NAMES :-
SWEET WILLIAM, WREAK,

harbour works. Mullet are taken usually by a seine -net as at Sennen. When many Mullet are enclosed in a seine, numbers will escape by leaping over the cork line in rapid succession. The trammel-net is probably the most effectual net to use for this fish, especially when backed up by another net at a distance of 3–4 feet away.

COD *(Gadus morhua)*:

The Cod is so well-known as a staple fish in the fish and chip trade as to hardly need description. Not a common fish on the Cornish coast, although some Cod are taken in trawls and some are taken on longlines.

LING *(Molva molva)*:

The Ling, as its name implies, is a long body-form fish and is a very voracious feeder. Ling have been known to be taken by swallowing other fish caught in trammel-nets and getting their own teeth enmeshed in the net. Many Ling are taken from wrecks and from the grounds near the Wolf Rock and the Isles of Scilly. In Cornwall they were formerly split, salted and dried for winter consumption. They take salt well and preserve quite easily.

HADDOCK *(Melanogrammus aeglefinus)*:

The average Haddock weighs only 2–3lbs, but may on occasion reach up to 8–10lbs. They will take most baits, but most are caught by trawl-nets. They are eaten fresh, but most are salted and smoked, and the 'Finnan Haddie' is well-known in most homes.

HAKE *(Merluccius merluccius)*:

The drift fishing for Pilchard and the hooking for Hake used to proceed at the same time and is managed in the following way. The Pilchard nets have been shot out in a straight line, the boat is then made fast to the last net and drifts along with the tide, and the lines, four or five in number, are then put out baited with fresh Pilchards. Hake usually range from 5–6lbs, up to 12lbs in weight, and because of their huge and sharp teeth strong gear and special hooks were made. The hooks were 2 inches from point to shank with an 8 inch shank. Haking, as it was known, was always practised at night for they do not feed well during daylight, and it was common for a Pilchard boat crewed by three or four men and a boy to catch 50 dozen Hake and 5,000 Pilchard in a single night.

SOLE *(Solea solea)*:

The Sole is generally taken with a trawl, but can be caught in a trammel, and is best fished close inshore at night. Special pockets are often meshed into trawls to ensure the capture of Soles as they attempt to swim back out of a trawl net.

Angler or Monk

CORNISH NAMES
MULVAINAH
FIDDLEFISH
FISHING FROG
ANGEL FISH
ROUND ROBIN
PESC MOLLAN

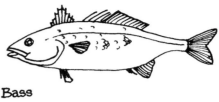

Bass

CORNISH NAMES :-
LUGALETH

Brill

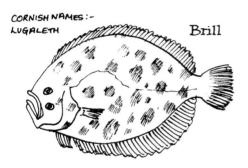

CORNISH NAMES :- BLACKJACK, RACER POLLACK
RAUNER POLLACK
RAUNING POLLACK

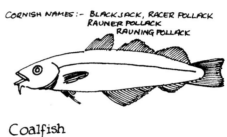

Coalfish

CORNISH NAMES :- BARFUS, BARVAS, BUCKYSOW
LOOBY (MaleCod) LOUNING (Spent Cod) LYLA (Spent Cod)
TOM LIN   TOW RAG (Dried Cod)

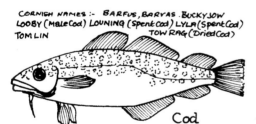

Cod

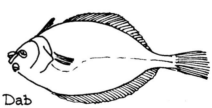

Dab

Dog Fish

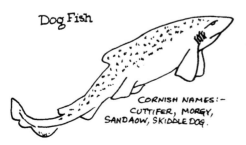

CORNISH NAMES :-
CUTTIFER, MORGY,
SANDAOW, SKIDDLE DOG.

CORNISH NAMES :- DRANIK, PICKADOG

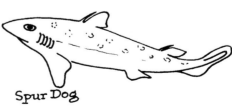

Spur Dog

PLAICE (*Pleuronectes platessa*):

Large quantities of Plaice are taken by the trawl. Formerly fished for in the Scillies by spearing from the bows of a punt, the trident-like spear being used both as paddle and harpoon.

TURBOT (*Scophthalmus maximus*):

This highly-prized fish frequents sandy banks around all parts of the British seas and is taken by trawlers and longliners. From 2–3,000 hooks are usually shot across the tide, the whole line extending about one mile. Up to ten miles of line may be carried by large boats engaged in this fishery.

BRILL (*Scophthalmus rhombus*):

The Brill, like the Turbot, is a bank-frequenting fish and is commonly caught in the trawl net. Occasionally caught on longlines, it is seldom caught by other methods. A good eating fish but not prized so highly as Turbot.

RED GURNARD (*Aspitrigla cuculus*):

So called because of the grunting sound they emit when taken out of the water. Gurnards are much in demand as bait for crab, lobster and crayfish.

CONGER (*Conger conger*):

The Conger is the largest of the eels and may attain a weight of 100lbs. It is found all round our coast and is usually caught on longlines. It is usually searched for on or near rocky ground or on wrecks. A Hake or Conger bat was sometimes carried to quieten these fish. It was usually fin-shaped, the tapered end doubling as a hook disgorger, and the business end used to club the eel once on the back of the head and twice at the termination of the fin on the abdomen – this being deemed sufficient to render the most truculent customer quite harmless!

SKATE (*Raja batis*):

This, and many other members of the ray family, are taken by trawl and longline on sandy and oozy grounds.

PILCHARD (*Sardina pilchardus*):

Formerly taken in huge numbers in seine-nets all around the Cornish coast and particularly at St Ives, this industry is now dead. The Pilchard, when it does enter British waters, does not come close enough to the land for the seine to be used. Many are still caught, however, by drift-net fishing. As well as being eaten fresh, the Pilchard was smoked, salted and canned.

HERRING (*Clupea harengus*):

Like the Pilchard industry, this fishery is now only a shadow of its former glory. The Herring is both trawled and caught in drift-nets.